D1083020

HONOR AND THE EPIC HERO

HONOR
AND THE
EPIC HERO

A Study of the Shifting Concept of Magnanimity
in Philosophy and Epic Poetry

Maurice B. McNamee, S.J.

HOLT, RINEHART AND WINSTON, INC.

New York

Imprimi potest: cum permissu superiorum
Societatis Jesu

NIHIL OBSTAT
Rev. Frederic C. Eckhoff
Censor Librorum Sancti Ludovici
Die 7, Mensis Januarii, 1959

IMPRIMATUR
Joseph E. Ritter, D.D.
Archiepiscopus Sancti Ludovici
Die 9, Mensis Januarii, 1959

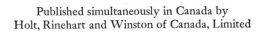

Published simultaneously in Canada by
Holt, Rinehart and Winston of Canada, Limited

To my sister,
Sister Mary Mauritia, O.S.F.

FALSTAFF I would 'twere bedtime, Hal, and all well.

PRINCE Why, thou owest God a death.

FALSTAFF 'Tis not due yet, I would be loath to pay Him before his day. What need I be so forward with him that calls not on me? Well, 'tis no matter. Honor pricks me on. Yea, but how if honor pricks me off when I come on? How then? Can honor set to a leg? No. Or an arm? No. Or take away the grief of a wound? No. Honor hath no skill in surgery, then? No. What is honor? A word. What is in that word honor? What is that honor? Air. A trim reckoning! Who hath it? He that died o' Wednesday. Doth he feel it? No. Doth he hear it? No. 'Tis insensible, then? Yea, to the dead. But will it not live with the living? No. Why? Detraction will not suffer it. Therefore I'll none of it. Honor is a mere scutcheon. And so ends my catechism.

I Henry IV, V, i, 125-143

Thus Falstaff esteems honor. And in a play in which Hotspur embodies the madness of the exaggerated pursuit of honor, Falstaff's view is not all jest. Both the fervid protestations of Hotspur and the jesting of Falstaff about honor are echoes of very ancient and ever-recurring attitudes in life and in letters.

One of the most helpful principles with which to approach the study of the major, early, literary genres is still Aristotle's time-worn principle of teleology. It is the principle which directs that the nature of anything is best revealed by a study of its end or purpose. Aristotle himself did a great deal to clarify the nature of art and literature in general and to distinguish it from the realm of the merely didactic and the propagandistic by insisting (against the opinion of his master Plato) that its primary end is not teaching but providing the pleasure of contemplation. And he actually laid the foundation for the whole theory and development of literary genres by further insisting that what distinguishes one literary kind from another is the diverse pleasure that each provides. Even his incomplete discussion of the major genres of tragedy, comedy, and the epic in his *Poetics* makes it quite apparent that the chief differences between these three types of literature in content and in form as he conceives them are the direct result of the very different types of pleasurable experience that each one aims at producing.

Tragedy and comedy are both built on incongruities, or departures from the usual and the normal. But they differ radically in the attitudes they immediately evoke toward the departures from the normal. Tragedy's immediate aim is to move us to tears while comedy's is to move us to laughter. The ultimate aim of both is to provide us with that pleasurable calm of which Aristotle speaks that comes from a new insight into the human situation, but they take very different roads to that destination. Tragedy first invites our pity for the erring hero while comedy excites our critical sense of his essential irrationality. But it is precisely these divergent dramatic purposes that determine what kind of situations and characters the tragedian and co-median will introduce into their respective works and also a great deal of the distinctive manner in which they present their material.

Since it is laughter that the comedian is attempting to evoke, he must have an alert sensitivity to what is laughable. It is the sudden departure from the normal, the usual, the expected that provokes a laugh. Why is it that we are apt instinctively to laugh at the sight of a man slipping on a banana peeling and sprawling gracelessly on the sidewalk? It is the sudden appre-hension of this very unusual position and movement of the human form that strikes us as funny. But if the same person were struck by an automobile and sent sprawling before us just as gracelessly, we would not be apt to laugh; we would more probably be shocked because of the greater likelihood of injury to the person in this kind of accident. The comedian, then, must know that it is the relatively painless aberration from the normal that is laughable. And it must also be some-thing from which we are relatively detached. If we were walk-ing down the street with our mother and she slipped on a banana peeling, the situation would again be shocking rather than laughable. This reveals the thin partition that separates laughter from tears, the comic from the tragic in human experi-ence. It also points up the fact that we are always somehow separate and aloof from the person or thing at which we laugh. There is a criticism implicit in every laugh. It is an instinctive way of ridiculing an aberration or abnormality. We consider ourselves in some way superior to the person at whom we laugh, at least in the aspect in which we find him laughable. When the aberration at which we are laughing is moral, the laugh is a judgment on the essential irrationality of all im-morality. But the aberration, even the moral aberration that is seen to be laughable, is not usually catastrophically serious. Like Puck in *Midsummer Night's Dream*, for a moment, we are separate, apart, and above offending man, and saying "What fools these mortals be." If we examine carefully our own feelings toward the situation or the character in the theater or in life at which we laugh, we will always find something of this distance between ourselves and them. We do not identify ourselves with the comic character at the moment in which we find him funny. If the comedian is to realize the purposes of his artistic creation, he has to be aware of all these demands of the truly comic and observe them.

The purpose of the tragedian also controls a great deal of his performance. The tragic spectacle is, like comedy, an incongruity, a departure from the normal and the usual, but, more often than not, a moral aberration for which the tragic character is personally responsible, and the consequence of which is more or less catastrophic to himself and others. Unlike the comic situation, tragedy is frought with pain and evokes, not laughter, but tears. It elicits our deepest sympathy and commiseration. We are not at all aloof and separate from the tragic spectacle but identify ourselves most closely with the tragic hero. It is the business of the tragedian, therefore, to build his characters with such convincing humanity that we see ourselves in them. We do not feel superior to the tragic character but very much one with him. We sympathize with him, and feel that there, but for the grace of God, go we. Unlike comedy, tragedy does not appeal to our critical sensitivity but rather to our emotional sensitivity to what it is like to be human. Horace Walpole has said somewhere that life is a comedy to those who think and a tragedy to those who feel. This is not to say that we suspend our judicious powers when we experience a tragic spectacle nor that we entirely outlaw our power of sympathy at human failure when we experience a comic spectacle, but it does point up a fundamental contrast between the two types of experience. Both the comedian and the tragedian must be keenly aware of these contrasts if they are to evoke to the full the pity and the laughter at which their respective media aim.

[ix]

The epic poet, too, is guided by his dominant purpose. Since the epic poem is built not upon incongruities in the actions of the main characters but upon the congruity between their actions and the ideals of the culture which the epic embodies, it is neither pity nor laughter that it aims at evoking but admiration. We are in countless ways invited to admire the epic hero for doing better and on a grander scale the things that are expected of the really great man in his society. Precisely because it is the man of heroic stature accomplishing truly great deeds that the epic holds up for our admiration we do not identify ourselves as closely with the epic as we do with the tragic hero. There is a certain awesome distance maintained between ourselves and the epic hero, but it is not, as in comedy, a critical but an approving distance. There is a kind of divinity that doth hedge an epic hero, and everything about the epic is calculated to make that apparent. The instinctive reaction to such exalted greatness is admiration or honor. Honor, in its most precise meaning, is merely the recognition of excellence wherever we find it, and it is the whole purpose of an epic to show forth the excellence of the epic hero so resplendently that our admiration for him is guaranteed. There is enough of the instinctive hero worshiper in all of us to make that not too difficult a task for the epic poet.

Every society, no matter how primitive, has its heroes whom it admires and honors; but what men find admirable and honorable in their heroes is, from society to society and from age to age, forever subtly changing. Since the epic is structured precisely to elicit our admiration for the hero, the great man of the society out of which it comes, it should be an excellent place in which to discover concretely what a nation's or a culture's concept of human greatness actually was. Its very spaciousness and diversity of episode should engender a confidence that it reveals rather fully what the culture it pictures considered particularly admirable and honorable in human achievement, because, unlike tragedy, the epic at its core is a success story and not a tale of failure. To discerning readers the epic has always performed that service; but, creatures of our own more immediate environment and experience, in the case of the epics as of so many other things that come to us from a distance in time and place, we sometimes tend to read into them our own values and attitudes instead of the values and attitudes of those by whom and for whom they were written. This is a danger we all encounter in reading anything from the past—a danger which must be minimized by a judicious study of the biography of the author where it is available and the historical background of the work itself. It is true, of course, that no literary work can ever mean exactly the same thing to us that it did to those for whom it was written in the first place, but that is not to say that a work of literature from the past is a completely blank check which we may fill in entirely according to our own lights and whims to the neglect of the intention of the author and of the literary, social, political, and religious milieu in which it was written. The intelligent reader and the responsible critic both have some obligation to try to get at the intention of the author and the reactions that he might have expected from his audience. They must not merely come up with a new creative work of their own occasioned by reading the work of the author under consideration, stimulating as that occupation may be to their own ego.

To avoid this rather irresponsible kind of subjectivity in his reading, the critic needs every help available. Interestingly enough, the philosophers provide him with some additional assistance for avoiding too subjective an interpretation of characters and situations in the great epics. In almost every epoch of civilization, philosophers have concerned themselves with the subject of human greatness or the heroic and frequently have analyzed minutely the basis of the honor paid the great men or heroes in the society in which they lived and thought. These analyses generally occur in the context of the philosophical discussions of the moral virtues. Aristotle began the tradition of placing the rational attitude toward personal honor high in the list of the virtues and of devoting a great deal of space and time to the consideration of the things for which a great man is honored in his own society. As a matter of fact, it was also Aristotle who first defined *magnanimity* as the virtue that is concerned with the rational attitude of a genuinely great man (great because pre-eminent in the practice of all the virtues honored in his society) toward his own personal honor and placed it above all the other virtues because it contained them all. Since the successive philosophical discussions of magnanimity embody the results of the most systematic and conscious exploration of the heroic or honorable in any given society, they can act as an additional cue to what that society's norms of human greatness actually were, at least in the society's more idealistic and self-analytical moments. If these philosophical analyses of the heroic or magnanimous correspond rather well with the image of magnanimity that we get by an independent internal analysis of an epic from the same culture, we have some additional assurance that we are not reading our own sets of human values and attitudes into eras and situations in which they more than likely did not obtain.

This, of course, does not mean that we should impose philosophical formulae, even though formulated by philosophers from the same cultural milieu as that of the epic poet, upon the epic under scrutiny. But if we find that the human values made concrete in the epic correspond rather closely to the ideal of human greatness formulated by the philosophers, we can have additional confidence that we are interpreting the epic characters and situations as would the audience for whom it was primarily composed. This generalization leaves room, to be sure, for literary works which are in revolt against or in advance of their cultural milieu in general and even of the age's own philosophical formulations of human greatness. In the case of the epic, however, as this book will show, the correspondence between literary concretion and philosophical formulation is more often than not remarkably exact. In some instances, notably in the case of Aristotle, the philosophical definition of the heroic or the magnanimous man follows centuries after the ideal had been incarnated in epic creations and is probably partly dependent upon them for some details. But whether these philosophical definitions of the honorable in man are the result of firsthand analyses of real men in action or of men as pictured in the nation's literary masterpieces or of a combination of both, they can be a decided help in interpreting the great epic characters and ideals more through the eyes of the author and of his audience than through our own.

It is with these relationships between the philosophical definitions of the magnanimous man and the great-souled man, as he is drawn for us by the epic poets, that this reexamination of some of the great epics of our Western tradition is concerned. The subsequent chapters will show, I think, that this juxtaposition of philosophical analysis and literary image of the great, magnanimous, or honorable man provides considerable help for achieving a more objective and historically accurate reading of the great epics. This is in no sense a study of sources or of influences. It is merely an attempt to show how a parallel study of a literary and a philosophical treatment of the heroic emanating from the same cultural milieu may help us to avoid the kind of literary criticism that can continue to see Achilles as a tragic character, Beowulf as predominantly pagan, and Satan as the hero of *Paradise Lost*.

M.B.M., S.J.

Saint Louis University
April, 1960

CONTENTS

PREFACE   vii

ONE   Aristotle's Magnanimous Man   1

TWO   Proud Achilles, the Noblest Achaean of Them All   8

THREE   Cicero's Magnanimous Man   40

FOUR   Dutiful Aeneas, the Typical Roman Hero   51

FIVE   The Christian Magnanimous Man   75

SIX   Beowulf, A Christian Hero   86

SEVEN   Magnanimity in Saint Augustine
and Saint Thomas Aquinas   118

EIGHT   Magnanimity in Spenser   137

NINE   Magnanimity in Milton   160

EPILOGUE   179

INDEX   183

[xv]

HONOR AND THE EPIC HERO

CHAPTER ONE

Aristotle's Magnanimous Man

> *"The Magnanimous man bears himself as he ought in the matter of both honour and dishonour. In fact, it goes without saying that the Magnanimous clearly have honour as their chief concern: since honour is what the truly great consider themselves specially to merit, and that in a very definite degree."*
> ARISTOTLE: *Nicomachean Ethics,* 1123b

One of the most striking and characteristic features of Greek culture is its self-centeredness. The Greek hero is individualistic, self-sufficient, and proud. And these qualities appear nowhere more clearly than in Aristotle's description of the magnanimous or great-souled man.[1] Great-mindedness or magnanimity he makes the crown of all the virtues because it presupposes excellence in all of them. It is the virtue that concerns itself with the right attitude towards the most important of all external goods—honor, or the recognition of one's own excellence.[2] Since the truly great-souled man is pre-eminent in all the virtues, he deserves the highest honor. Therefore any honor that he demands is only what is his due; he can never be excessive in his claims for honor or recognition. This is a unique situation in the catalogue of Aristotelian virtues. As we know, Aristotle conceived of virtue as a mean between the opposite extremes of excess and defect. Magnanimity is the only virtue in his list that cannot lapse into vice through excess. For Aristotle, no truly great-souled man can claim more honor than is his due. It would also seem clear, from Aristotle's discussion of this virtue, that the great-souled man must demand the highest possible acclaim; it is not a privilege that he may or may not exercise, but a solemn duty. If he actually has the excellence of soul that deserves the highest recognition, failure to demand that recognition would be a mark of weakness, a sign of pusillanimity or small-mindedness.[3] And small-mindedness was despised by the Greeks as a defect, a lack of courage to demand one's due mead of honor. There was hardly anyone, in fact, more contemptible in the eyes of a Greek than such a weak-willed individual.

The self-centeredness and self-sufficiency of this Aristotelian virtue is made even more apparent by what is said about the proper relationships between the magnanimous man and his fellow men. In the first place it is pointed out that he must not allow his life to become centered on any other individual with the possible exception of a friend equal to himself.[4] Conscious of his own excellence and superiority, the magnanimous man has little regard for the praise of those inferior to himself; but he is not at all indifferent to the opinion of those who are as great or nearly as great as he. The approval of the latter, in fact, is the special recognition that he considers particularly his due. For a like reason, he resents the criticism of the great, but is indifferent to that of his inferiors. He bears himself in a haughty manner toward the great lest the slightest impression be left that he is inferior to them, but he is condescending toward his inferiors because it is obvious that they *are* his inferiors. He is very mindful of favors that he has done for others because the ability to help others reveals his superiority to them; but he is quick to forget favors done for him because favors received suggest his inferiority to the doer.

The same self-absorption is evident in Aristotle's description of the magnanimous man's attitude toward wealth and power. He does not set his heart on either power or riches for themselves, but he esteems them for the honor that accrues to their possession. He is also conscious of the fact that, for the unenlightened many, riches and power are more easily discernible than the virtue which is his true claim to respect. Particularly revealing is Aristotle's attitude toward the contempt that the truly magnanimous man and the merely rich and powerful man have for their inferiors. The real difference, for Aristotle, is that the contempt of the truly great-minded man is justified by the facts because he really *is* superior, whereas that of the merely rich and powerful is not justified because he is only *apparently* superior. The interesting point of the contrast is the fact that the contempt of the magnanimous man for his inferiors is defended as one of his rights.[5]

In the early period of every cultural epoch, some of the most important, and sometimes almost the exclusive claims for honor, are physical prowess and courage displayed on the battlefield. Aristotle's magnanimous man is not indifferent to these sources of glory. Satisfied with the recognition given his general pre-eminence, he does not court trifling dangers, nor does he love even great dangers on or off the battlefield; but once he is challenged by a threat that is worth his mettle and it becomes apparent that to avoid battle or the risk of death would discredit him in the eyes of others, he goes into battle and fights almost recklessly. There is something, Aristotle insists, more valuable to him than life itself—his honor and reputation.[6] It is not the glory of the cause nor the help he might be to others that galvanizes him into action but the fear of having his own reputation besmirched with the accusation of cowardice. This obsession with one's personal honor and fame on the part of the Greek hero is more intelligible if we remember that the Greek notion of a hereafter was very vague and uninviting. In the absence of anything very promising to look forward to in the afterlife, the Greek was concerned to guarantee the perdurance of his name and fame after death by the deeds done while he still lived.[7]

Still other facets of the self-centeredness of the Greek virtue of magnanimity are revealed in the contrasts which Aristotle makes between the truly magnanimous man whose

[3]

pre-eminent virtues justify his claim to supreme honor and the man who makes that claim unjustifiably. The lesser virtue of the mediocre man gives him the right only to a commensurate honor. But unlike the truly magnanimous man, he can lay claim to honors beyond his deserts and become the ambitious or vain man. He can also lack the courage to demand even the lesser honor due him and become the pusillanimous man.[8] If the truly magnanimous man who failed to demand the honor due him is contemptible, then, says Aristotle, this man is beneath contempt. But more interesting, as further revealing the emphasis placed on this pursuit of honor by the Greeks, is Aristotle's remark that of the two, a failure by defect in this mediocre man is more to be condemned than failure by excess. Not to claim the honor due one is worse than claiming more than one's due.[9]

Even Aristotle's discussion of such minor considerations as the possessions, gait, voice, and speech of the magnanimous man reinforces the central selfishness of his character. He prefers useless, beautiful objects to practical, useful ones because the possession of the latter would suggest a dependence upon them, and he is loath to admit his dependence upon anything. He assumes a slow, dignified gait because any show of haste would suggest a lack of self-assurance. And, finally, he speaks in a low, steadily modulated voice, because a high-pitched, unmodulated voice would show undue excitement; and there is nothing really great enough outside himself to excite the magnanimous man.

The point of interest for us in this whole discussion is that it is these very self-centered qualities of Aristotle's magnanimous man that form the specific bases of the honor paid to him. In this connection W. D. Ross justly remarks:

> There are admirable traits among those here depicted, but as a whole the picture is an unpleasing one; it is an anticipation of the Stoic sage without his self-abasement before the ideal of duty. The offensiveness of the picture is miti-

gated, but not removed, if we remember that the man who behaves like this is supposed to have, to start with, the highest possible merits. Nor can we fairly suppose that the account of this virtue, unlike that of the others, is ironical, or is a mere exposition of popular views. The passage simply betrays somewhat nakedly the self-absorption which is the bad side of Aristotle's ethics.[10]

It betrays not only the bad side of Aristotle's ethics but the bad side of the whole Greek humanistic ideal—an exaggerated individualism and selfishness.

Plato, in *The Republic*, had shown himself quite aware of the evil social and political effects of this exaggerated Greek individualism, and he makes unselfishness the most important qualification of his governing class. But we must remember that *The Republic* does not represent the actual Greek attitude or practice, but rather an ideal presented as a corrective to what Plato considered actual Greek aberrations. And so far was he from making his ideal prevail that Aristotle, his most prominent pupil, here presents the very traits that Plato wished eradicated from the Greek character as the traits of his magnanimous man. Aristotle elevates what Plato recognized, with almost Christian insight, as vices into "the crown of all the virtues." In the next chapter, we shall see that it was Aristotle's concept of the great man, and not Plato's, that, centuries before the time of either philosopher, had operated in the great epic hero, Achilles.

NOTES

[1] Aristotle's discussion of magnanimity occurs in his *Ethica Nicomachea*, Book IV, Sections 3 and 4 (1123a-34, 1125b-25). This summary is based on the translation by W. D. Ross, which occurs in *The Works of Aristotle*, Vol. IX, translated and edited by J. A. Smith and W. D. Ross (New York: Oxford University Press, 1925). All future references to the *Ethics* will be to this edition.

[2] This is Aristotle's own description of the magnanimous man:

"Now the man is thought to be proud [magnanimous] who thinks himself worthy of great things, being worthy of them . . . the proud [magnanimous] man, then is an extreme in respect of the greatness of his claims, but a mean in respect of the rightness of them" (1123b-13). Ross, like some other Aristotelian scholars, is here translating μεγαλόψυχος (great-souled) as "proud" because pride with all its connotations of self-centeredness comes closest to the virtue that Aristotle calls μεγαλοψυχία (magnanimity or greatminded-ness).

3 "The man who thinks himself worthy of less than he is really worthy of is unduly humble, whether his deserts be great or moderate, or his deserts be small but his claims yet smaller. And the man whose deserts are great would seem *most* unduly humble; for what would he have done if they had been less" (1123b-8)?

4 "He must be unable to make his life revolve round another, unless it be a friend" (1125a). And even in the case of a friend the relationship, as Aristotle describes it elsewhere in the *Nicomachean Ethics*, is not unself-centered. Even the third and highest degree of friendship in Aristotle is at least partly measured by the higher pleasure and utility that the friend, as a *good* man like to or equal to oneself, provides to the befriended. Aristotle actually says that for the magnanimous man the love for a friend for his own lovable-ness is really a love of oneself reflected in the corresponding good-ness and excellence of the friend.

5 "Disdainful and insolent, however, even those who have such goods [goods of fortune, noble birth, riches, and power] become. For without virtue it is not easy to bear gracefully the goods of fortune; and, being unable to bear them, and thinking themselves superior to others, they despise others and themselves do what they please. They imitate the proud [magnanimous] man without being like him, and this they do where they can; so they do not act virtuously, but they do despise others. *For the proud* [magnanimous] *man despises justly* (since he thinks truly), but the many do so at random" (1124a-30). The italics are mine. Notice that, according to Aristotle, the magnanimous man despises too, but justly, because the object of his contempt *is* inferior to him.

6 "He does not run into trifling dangers, nor is he fond of danger, because he honours few things; but he will face great dangers, and when he is in danger he is unsparing of his life, knowing that

[6]

there are conditions on which life is not worth having" (1124b-7).

⁷ Fear of death was one of the predominant weaknesses of the Greeks. In their gravestone sculpture they tried to ignore death by representing the dead engaged in some characteristic activity of life. One of Plato's criticisms of the poets in *The Republic* is that they paint such an unpleasant picture of the afterlife that they increase men's fear of death. He refers explicitly to Achilles' declaration in the underworld that so dismal is life among the shades of the underworld that he would sooner be the servant of the poorest landless shepherd on earth than the king of the underworld. So important did it seem to Plato to overcome this fear of death—that he invented the myth of Er about the hereafter to offset it. This myth is startlingly close to the Christian notion of the hereafter, but there is little evidence that it became current among the Greeks. They continued to place much more emphasis on perdurance through the fame of great deeds done here than through a life hereafter.

⁸ The difference between the position of magnanimity and the parallel unnamed virtue of the mediocre man in reference to the extremes of excess and defect is best clarified diagrammatically:

Defect	*Virtue*	*Excess*
Pusillanimity	*Magnanimity* (great-souled man)	none
Pusillanimity	*Unnamed virtue* (mediocre man)	unwarranted ambition or vanity

⁹ "Undue humility is more opposed to pride than vanity is; for it is both commoner and worse" (1125a-33).

¹⁰ W. D. Ross, *Aristotle* (London: Methuen & Co., Ltd., 1949), p. 208. Reprinted by permission of the publishers.

CHAPTER TWO

Proud Achilles,
the Noblest Achaean of Them All

*"And the son of Peleus pressed on in search of glory,
bespattering his unconquerable hands with gore."*

HOMER: *Iliad,* XX

ACHILLES: *"Put me on earth again, and I would rather
be a serf in the house of some landless man, with little enough for himself to live on, than king of all
these dead men that have done with life."*

HOMER: *Odyssey,* XI

To many modern readers, Achilles may appear to be proud,
selfish, egotistical, and unbelievably stubborn, and therefore
deserving of neither admiration nor sympathy. To some modern critics, on the other hand, he seems to be essentially a tragic
character, who, by an excess of anger and hurt pride, brings
about the death of his dearest friend and of dozens of his
fellow Achaeans.[1] The Greeks themselves, for whom *The Iliad*
was written, would probably have reacted to his character
quite differently. So far from condemning him as overly proud
or pitying him as a tragic figure,[2] they would more probably
have admired him as a rather good embodiment of their notion
of a hero. They would very likely have considered the final
outcome of the poem as much a triumph for Achilles as was
the victory over the suitors for Odysseus. The character of

[8]

Achilles himself and the motivation of the central action of the poem are such a perfect exemplification of the magnanimous man as Aristotle describes him that we can be relatively sure that Aristotle had Achilles in mind when he phrased that description, as he had the actual heroes of the great Greek tragedians in mind when he discussed the nature of the tragic hero in his *Poetics*. The character and actions of the hero of *The Iliad* are concrete evidence of the distance between the Greek concept of honor and our own.

For, after all, what is the central action of *The Iliad?* In its baldest terms it is simply this: The great Achilles has been dishonored before the whole Greek host by King Agamemnon, and so important is his honor to Achilles that he is willing to sacrifice half the Greek army to reassert his superiority over the King. The details of the story are familiar. The Greek army was being decimated with a plague by Apollo. The god had been angered because Agamemnon refused to restore to her father, a priest of Apollo, the damsel Chryseis, whom Agamemnon had taken to himself as part of the spoils of war. To placate the god and save his army from the plague, Agamemnon finally agrees to restore the girl to her father, but consoles himself for the loss by seizing Briseis. This damsel had been given to Achilles as a very special gift of honor in recognition of that incomparable hero's prowess in conquering and sacking innumerable cities. Achilles would not have been so mortally offended if Agamemnon had stripped him of all the rich booty that fell to him from previous exploits; but it was a black, unforgivable insult to take away this girl who had been given to him as a special public mark of honor in recognition of his superior prowess and valor.[3] It was tantamount to Agamemnon's saying that Achilles was inferior to him, and this was a humiliation at the hands of the King, a man whose opinion counted in the eyes of men, that the great Achilles simply could not brook. He withdrew from battle, and remained aloof until it was quite apparent to Agamemnon and the whole Greek host that without him they were helpless to save themselves from destruction at the hands of the Trojans. We are left in no possible doubt about this dominant motive of Achilles for his withdrawal from battle and for his stubborn aloofness. As he withdraws he flings this taunt at Agamemnon:

> "The day is coming when the Achaeans one and all will miss me sorely, and you in your despair will be powerless to help them as they fall in their hundreds to Hector killer of men. Then will you tear your heart out in remorse for having treated the best man in the expedition with contempt."—I, p. 29.

Later, pleading with his goddess-mother, Thetis, to win over Zeus to his course, he says:

> "Persuade him, if you can, to help the Trojans, to fling the Achaeans back on their ships, to pen them in against the sea and slaughter them. That would teach them to appreciate their King. That would make imperial Agamemnon son of Atreus realize what a fool he was to insult the noblest of them all."—I, pp. 33-34.

Later, when the Trojans are already threatening the very ships of the Achaeans, Achilles sees it as an answer to his prayer. He remarks to Patroclus:

> "My dear prince and my heart's delight, at last I see the Achaeans gathering at my knees to abase themselves, for they are in desperate straits."—XI, p. 213.

In this central action of the poem there is no tragic defeat for Achilles; he gets exactly what he wants and stands at the end of the poem completely victorious. In the last scene, in which we see Achilles and Agamemnon together at the funeral games for Patroclus, Achilles is friendly and even condescending toward Agamemnon. He could now afford to be, because his own superiority over the king had been completely vindicated. If we wish to see this central motivation and action of the poem as the Greeks saw it, we would do well to see it in the light of Aristotle's emphasis on the supreme importance of personal honor in the life of the hero. If we look carefully, it becomes apparent that every detail of the story, as it touches Achilles, gyrates around his quest for and insistence on his own personal honor and fame above all other values.

In the first place, Achilles is certainly given heroic stature in the poem. He is described as superior to everyone in the whole Greek host, Agamemnon included. With the possible exception of Telemonian Ajax, there is no one in the whole Greek army who can match him in sheer strength and physical prowess. Ajax, however, is more brawny than brainy; while Achilles has an intelligence that matches his towering strength. On the battlefield he has no peer for indomitable courage and ruthlessness. His beauty of physique is so great that it frequently reveals him to be what he is—half divine, since he was the son of the goddess Thetis. As became the "greatest Achaean of them all," there was nothing about his circumstances that was mediocre. His armor surpassed that of all the other Achaeans, fashioned as it was by the divine hands of Hephaestus himself. His spear was so tremendous that no one except himself could wield it. It took three men to draw the tremendous bar to the gate of his enclosure, but he, of course, could flick it open or shut with one hand. And so it went. Even his horses were superior to all others. They were, in fact, also half divine; and one of them, Xanthus, had the power of speech, which he used, naturally, to praise his master and lament his fated early death.

Achilles' pre-eminence is highlighted not only by the many excellent qualities that are attributed to him personally but also by the contrasts that are drawn between him and other great characters in the story. The central action, we have seen, is designed to demonstrate his superiority over Agamemnon. Ajax is described as mighty and devastating in combat, the greatest battler of the Achaeans, but only in the absence of Achilles.

Odysseus is conceded to excel in wily counsels, or as Achilles himself puts it, "in the war of words"; but he is frequently pictured as something less than eager for the gory business of the battlefield where Achilles is most at home. Menelaus is almost the perfect example of the ambitious man as Aristotle defines him. He is mediocre in almost every respect, but is forever volunteering or eager and ambitious to take up challenges that are beyond his capacities, not without an eye to the glory that would be his if he succeeded in these exploits. He has to be frequently reminded of his limitations and gently shown his place even by his brother Agamemnon. But his very mediocrity is a foil against which Achilles' superiority shines the brighter.[4] Achilles' heroic stature also grows by contrast with even the greatest of Trojan warriors. Aenaes is described by the god Poseidon as truly magnanimous, but the old sea-god recognizes that he is simply no match for Achilles and tells him so as he snatches him from a premature death at the "man-killing" hands of Achilles.

"Which of the gods told you to fight with the proud Achilles," Poseidon chides, "who is not only a better soldier than you but a greater favourite with the immortals? If ever you come up against that man, withdraw at once, or you will find yourself in Hades' Halls before your time. But when he is dead and gone, you can boldly play your part in the front line, for no one else on the Achaean side is going to kill you."—XX, pp. 374-375.

But the most flattering foil for Achilles' greatness, of course, is his Trojan opponent Hector. Since Achilles is to win his greatest fame in the story by defeating Hector, Homer had to give that Trojan warrior heroic stature, and he certainly succeeded in doing so. In the absence of Achilles Hector was the most formidable warrior on the plains of Troy.[5] He carried everything before him. But his very pre-eminence and the chaos he created in the Greek ranks only served to augment the glory of Achilles when he rejoined the fray and defeated the redoubtable Hector. Thus both the strength and the weakness of Greek and Trojan heroes alike were made to highlight the towering superiority of "the noblest of the Achaeans."

Achilles himself was the last to deny this superiority; indeed, he was keenly aware of it and asserted it on every possible occasion. We have already heard him bitterly taunting Agamemnon for treating "the best man in the expedition with contempt" (I, pp. 29, 34). When he is threatening to launch his ships and sail home to Phthia, at the moment when Hector is threatening the very ships of the Greeks, he reminds Odysseus that "when [he Achilles] took the field with the Achaeans nothing would have induced Hector to throw his men into battle at any distance from the city walls. He came no farther than the Scaean Gate and the oak-tree, where he took me on alone one day, and was lucky to get home alive" (IX, p. 170). In his conversation with his mother Thetis about going back into battle to revenge the death of his friend Patroclus, he laments that he, "the best man in all the Achaean force, the best in battle, defeated only in the war of words," has proven a broken reed to his friend (XVIII, p. 339). He seldom, in fact, ever refers to himself except in superlatives, and none of his auditors, human or divine, ever deny that they are justified.

Achilles shows this consciousness of his own superiority not only by his own statements and presumptions about himself but also by his attitude toward all his fellow Achaeans. His relationships with all of them are very much those of the magnanimous man as Aristotle later described him. With inferiors like Ajax and Odysseus, for instance, he can be quite friendly and condescending,[6] but toward Agamemnon, the recognized leader of the whole Greek army who has dishonored him, he is consistently haughty and insolent.[7] Even his relationship with Patroclus fits the Aristotelian pattern. Aristotle said that the magnanimous man "must be unable to make his life revolve round another, unless it be a friend." [8] Patroclus was such a friend. But even toward Patroclus Achilles' attitude was not entirely unselfish. He did not look

[13]

on Patroclus as an equal but as a lesser version of himself in whose good qualities he saw himself reflected. So he looked upon the death of Patroclus as another insult flung by Hector at himself. Patroclus, we recall, went out to battle in Achilles' armor, and the driving motive of Hector in slaying him was to have the honor of capturing the armor of the famed Achilles (XVIII, p. 334). It was not *all* an unselfish grief for his friend that so infuriated Achilles at Hector's slaying of Patroclus.

Achilles' personal honor, in fact, was behind almost every move, great and small, that he made throughout the whole *Iliad*. As we have already seen, he withdrew from battle in boiling wrath because he had been dishonored by Agamemnon. He remained aloof from the battlefield until, with the whole Greek army and the very ships on the brink of annihilation by the Trojans, it had become painfully apparent to Agamemnon and all the Greeks how completely dependent they were upon him for victory. His answer to the second delegation from Agamemnon makes his position and his motives perfectly clear.

"My blood boils when I think of what happened, and the vile way in which Atreides treated me in public, like some disreputable outcast. Go now, and report my decisions. I will not think again of bloodshed and war, until Prince Hector, son of the wise Priam, reaches the huts and ships of the Myrmidons, killing Argives as he comes, and destroys the fleet by fire. I have a notion that, however furious his attack may be, Hector will be brought up short, here by my own hut and my own black ship."—IX, p. 178.

In other words, he planned on waiting for the moment which would be most humiliating to Agamemnon and which would redound most to his own glory. Later, when the Trojans are already at the ships, we hear him remarking with obvious satisfaction to Patroclus:

[14]

"My dear prince and my heart's delight, at last I see the Achaeans gathering at my knees to abase themselves, for they are in desperate straits."—XI, p. 213.

Finally, persuaded by Patroclus to do something to save the ships from going up in smoke, he consents to allow Patroclus to go into battle in his armor, as he gloats over the helplessness of the Achaeans without him.

"The whole town of Troy [he says] seems to have taken heart and turned out against us. And no wonder, when they do not see the vizor of *my* helmet flashing in the foreground. They would soon take to their heels and fill the gullies with their dead, if King Agamemnon would treat me as a friend." —XVI, p. 294.

Achilles is confident that, if he merely sends Patroclus into the battle in his armor, the Trojans will scatter in panic. But before he allows Patroclus to go into battle to save the ships, he cautions him about just how far he is to go. He must not allow his head to be turned by success in the fray and carry on the battle against Hector alone. That honor is to be reserved for Achilles himself. He is blatantly explicit on the point. His sending Patroclus is part of a maneuver to reflect credit not on Patroclus, but on himself:

"But listen while I tell you exactly how far to go, in order to induce the whole Danaan army to value and respect me as they should and to send the lovely lady back to me, with ample compensation too. Return to me, directly you have swept the Trojans from the ships. Even if Zeus the Thunderer offers you the chance of winning glory for yourself, you must not seize it. You must not fight without *me* against those warlike Trojans—you would only make me cheaper."—XVI, p. 294.

[15]

And then he makes a remark which reveals the colossal proportions of his egoism, and the degree to which he puts his own glory above the welfare of his fellow Achaeans:

> "Ah, Father Zeus, Athene and Apollo, how happy I should be if not a Trojan got away alive, not one, and not an Argive either, if we two survived the massacre to pull down Troy's holy diadem of towers single-handed!"—XVI, p. 294.

Egoism can hardly go farther than that, but with Achilles it does, as we shall see.

Patroclus, in the event, forgot his restrictions, pursued the Trojans to their very walls, and was slain at the hands of Hector. This enraged Achilles beyond measure; and he decided that this was the time to revenge the death of his friend and to cover himself with glory by slaying single-handed the greatest of the Trojans who until now had had the whole Greek army in rout. He was so impatient to get at the Trojans that he would not even wait for his new coat of armor. He rushed out on the plain and gave out with such blood-curdling battle cries that the whole Trojan army was petrified with terror, and some of their best men committed suicide on the spot. When he finally consented to delay the combat until his goddess Mother had procured a new suit of armor for him from the forge of Hephaestus, he told her that he was obsessed now not mainly by the thought of revenge nor with the thought of his own predestined death here on the windy plains of Troy but with the thought of the undying fame that would be his as the slayer of the matchless Hector. These are his own words:

> "I will go now and seek out Hector, the destroyer of my dearest friend. As for my death, when Zeus and the other deathless gods appoint it, let it come. . . . But for the moment, glory is my aim. I will make these Trojan women and deep-bosomed daughters of Dardanus wipe the tears from their tender cheeks with both their hands as they raise the dirge, to teach them just how long I have been absent from the war."—XVIII, p. 340.[9]

[16]

As a last resource, Odysseus had appealed to this very motive when he tried to persuade Achilles to get back into the battle. Achilles had already refused to accept the gift of the humbled Agamemnon, and Odysseus shrewdly couches his final appeal in these words:

> ". . . if your hatred for Atreides, gifts and all, outweighs every other consideration, do have some pity on the rest of the united Achaeans, lying dead-beat in their camp. They will honour you like a god. Indeed, you could cover yourself with glory in their eyes, for now is the time when you could get Hector himself. He fancies that he has no match among all the Danaans whom the ships brought here, and he may even venture near you, in his insensate fury."—IX, p. 169.

The wily Odysseus was showing his real shrewdness in making this final appeal to Achilles' love of glory, but Achilles was not yet sure the time was ripe for reaping the fullest harvest of glory. He would not come back until he had humiliated Agamemnon to the dust. "First he must pay in kind for the bitter humiliation I endured," is his reply (IX, p. 171).

When Achilles finally did go into battle against Hector, blazing like a god in his new armor, it was quite apparent that his dominant motive was not "pity for the rest of the Achaeans" but rather the glory that would be his forever as the slayer of the great Hector. And he made it clear that he did not intend to share that glory with anyone else. When he was in pursuit of the fleeing Hector around the walls of Troy, he signaled to his men

> by movements of his head that they were not to shoot at the quarry, for fear that he might be forestalled and one of them might win renown by striking Hector with an arrow. —XXII, p. 402.

When he has finally brought Hector low with a well-aimed thrust of his spear, he taunts his victim with these words:

[17]

"Hector, no doubt you fancied as you stripped Patroclus that you would be safe. You never thought of me: I was too far away. You were a fool. Down by the hollow ships there was a man far better than Patroclus in reserve, the man who has brought you low."—XXII, p. 406.

With that Achilles dealt the deathblow to the prostrate Hector. Achilles' followers looked in amazement at "the size and marvelous good looks of Hector," and each of them tried to steal some of Achilles' honor by thrusting his spear into the body of the mightiest of the Trojans. But Achilles reminded them that Hector had once been more formidable to them all with the words "Hector is easier to handle now than when he set the ships on fire" (XXII, p. 407). Achilles, now exultant, had the Achaeans take up the body of Hector and carry it back to the ships as they sang with him this song of triumph: "We have won great glory. We have killed the noble Hector, who was treated like a god in Troy" (ibid.). And to savor his triumph over the great Trojan, Achilles proceeded to subject his dead body to the indignity of being tied to the rear of his chariot and dragged in the dust about the walls of Troy and the barrow of Patroclus.

Achilles had at last attained his greatest wish, even if he had paid for it with the death of so many Achaeans, including that of his dearest friend. He had humiliated Agamemnon, who had come crawling to him to save the Achaeans from destruction, and he had won imperishable glory for himself by slaying the mighty Hector. As something of an outward symbol of his triumph over Agamemnon, the gifts which the king had promised to him if he came to the aid of the Achaeans were now brought to him with all due ceremony; and they included the damsel Briseis, that special prize of honor whose seizure had occasioned his unquenchable wrath (XIX, p. 361).

The Achilles we see at the funeral games of Patroclus is a friendly, condescending Achilles. He abstains from entering the chariot race because his horses are grieving over the death of Patroclus, but not without reminding the contestants that on any other occasion he would win against any challengers. In any event, he has just won a much bigger contest, so he can afford to be indifferent about these much smaller stakes. In like spirit he doubles the prize for Antilochus because Antilochus had made the complimentary remark that Odysseus is a hard man to overcome in a race—"for anyone but Achilles" (XXIII, p. 433). He awards a prize to Agamemnon without letting him contend for it and graciously compliments him on his superior prowess as a spearsman. He can afford to be gracious even to Agamemnon now, since he has so completely vindicated his own superiority over him.[10] But it is his own glory that remains uppermost in his mind until the last. He bids his followers construct a modest barrow for Patroclus now, but later a mighty one for himself and his friend when he has followed Patroclus into Hades. "As for his barrow," he says, "I do not ask you to construct a very large one, something that is seemly but no more. Later you can build a big and high one, you Achaeans that are left in the well-found ships when I am gone" (XXIII, pp. 418-419).

If we follow Achilles into the underworld as Homer does in *The Odyssey*, we will see that Achilles in Hades is the same old Achilles that we have come to know in *The Iliad*. When Odysseus visits the underworld, he meets the shade of Achilles there and hales him as the

"most fortunate man that ever was or will be! For in the old days when you were on earth, we Argives honoured you as though you were a god; and now, down here, you are a mighty prince among the dead. For you, Achilles, Death should have lost his sting."—XI, p. 184.[11]

But Achilles takes a less glowing view of his present situation:

"Put me on earth again [he says] and I would rather be a serf in the house of some landless man, with little enough for himself to live on, than king of all these dead men that have done with life."—XI, p. 184.

[19]

What he is really interested in is his son on earth. Is he living up to the reputation of his celebrated father? "Did he follow me to the war and play a leading part or not" (XI, p. 184)? And what about his old father? How is he now without his son to protect him? These are the interests of Achilles in Hades; and as he shouts these questions at Odysseus a spark of the old boastful Achilles flashes out for a moment:

> "If I could return [he says] for a single day to my father's house with the strength I then enjoyed, I would make those who injure him and rob him of his rights shrink in dismay before my might and my unconquerable hands."—XI, p. 184.

About Achilles' father Odysseus knows nothing, but about his son he can be very reassuring. He is a son of whom Achilles can be proud. He gives Achilles a glowing account of the prowess of the lad. It would seem that he gives promise of even bettering his father in one area, since Odysseus says he is bettered in debate by only the wise old Nestor and himself. Achilles lets that pass without comment, but he listens eagerly as Odysseus describes his son's prowess on the battlefield.

> "That impetuous spirit of his [says Odysseus] gave place to none, and he would sally out beyond the foremost. Many was the man he brought down in mortal combat. I could not tell you all the people he killed in battle for the Argives. . . . When we Argive captains took our places in the wooden horse Epeius made, and it rested solely with me to throw our ambush open or to keep it shut, all the other Danaan chieftains and officers were wiping the tears from their eyes and every man's legs were trembling beneath them, but not once did I see your son's fine colour change to pallor nor catch him brushing a tear from his cheek. On the contrary he begged me time and again to let him sally from the Horse and kept fumbling eagerly at his sword-hilt and his heavy spear in his keenness to fall on the Trojans."—XI, p. 185.

[20]

Here was a son after the heart of the mighty Achilles himself. This news of home was a bright spot for Achilles in the darkness of the underworld.

> "The soul of Achilles, [said Odysseus] whose feet had been so fleet on earth, passed with great strides down the meadow of asphodel, rejoicing in the news I had given him of his son's renown."—*Ibid*.

To have such a son was the next best thing to being among the living himself, where he could be winning undying fame with his "unconquerable hands."

We catch another glimpse of Achilles in the underworld when the souls of the suitors arrive there. They find him in conversation with the shade of Agamemnon. He is condoling with the king for his inglorious death at the hands of the faithless Clytemnestra. Agamemnon agrees that Achilles' death was by far the happier one

> . . . "in Troyland far away from Argos, with the flower of the Trojan and Achaean forces falling round you in battle for your corpse. There in a whirl of dust you lay, great even in your fall, thinking no longer of charioteer's delights."— XXIV, p. 352.

Then, after relating in great detail all the funeral honors paid to Achilles by Achaeans and gods alike, Agamemnon describes the glorious mound that was built for him.

> "We soldiers of the mighty Argive force built up a great and glorious mound, on a foreland jutting out over the broad waters of the Hellespont, so that it might be seen far out at sea by the sailors of to-day and future ages. Then, in the middle of the lists where the Achaean champions were to test their skill, your mother placed the magnificent prizes she had asked the gods to give. You must often have attended royal funerals yourself, when the young men strip and make ready

for the games by which they honour their dead king, but the splendid prizes offered in *your* honour by the divine Thetis of the Silver Feet would have struck you as the most wonderful you had ever seen. For the gods loved you very dearly. Thus even death, Achilles, did not destroy your glory and the whole world will honour you for ever."—XXIV, p. 353.

What satisfaction it was to be hearing all this from Agamemnon. Achilles had once been given a choice: to go home to Phthia and live to a peaceful but inglorious old age, or to remain at Troy and die an early death but gain immortal fame. He pretended for a time to have chosen home and the peaceful old age; but it was only a pretense.[12] His real and ultimate choice was death and immortal fame on the plains of Troy. He had lived for glory; he had died for glory; and now Agamemnon was telling him that not even death had destroyed his glory. The whole world would honor him forever. That was all that Achilles had ever asked for in life.

It should also be noted that it was not just any kind of glory that interested Achilles. He was even willing to concede that he was worsted by Odysseus in debate, in the "war of words"; but he would yield to no one in what he considered the far more important war of swords.[13] Nor was it just any kind of battle that he was interested in, but only one which he considered a real challenge to his superior prowess. That is why he was so anxious to reserve the combat with Hector to himself. Aristotle had observed that the magnanimous man

> does not run into trifling dangers, nor is he fond of danger, because he honours few things; but he will face great dangers, and when he is in danger he is unsparing of his life, knowing that there are conditions on which life is not worth having.[14]

This is only partly the code of Achilles. It is true that he despised small dangers as not a sufficient challenge to his superior powers, and that honor on the battlefield meant more to

him than life; but we have a feeling all through *The Iliad* that
in Achilles we are dealing with a more primitive ideal than
even that described by Aristotle. Achilles, of course, did love
battle chiefly as a means of winning undying fame; but he also
seemed to have an unholy delight in the sheer butchery of the
battlefield. He appeared to be happiest when his "unconquerable hands were bespattered with gore." When he was finally
ready to go into battle against the Trojans he had no time to
eat nor did he wish to allow the weary Achaean soldiers a
respite for food; his one thought was of "blood and slaughter
and the groans of dying men" (XIX, p. 359). The following
are only two from among many passages that show his delight
in the bloody business of the battlefield. While Achilles is slaying Trojans right and left, Tros, a young Trojan warrior,
clasps his knees and begs for mercy, to no avail:

> Achilles [says Homer] was not kind or tender-hearted, but a
> man of fierce passions; and when Tros in his eagerness to
> plead for mercy put his hands on his knees, he struck him in
> the liver with his sword. The liver came out and drenched his
> lap with dark blood. He swooned, and night descended on
> his eyes.—XX, p. 378.

But Tros is just one among many in the slaughter:

> Achilles then went up to Mulius and struck him on the ear
> with his javelin, so hard that the bronze point came out at
> the other ear. The next was Echeclus, son of Agenor. Achilles
> caught him full on the head with a stroke of his hilted sword
> —the blood made the whole blade warm. . . . Deucalion
> next. Achilles pierced his forearm with the bronze point of
> his spear, just where the sinews of the elbow are attached.
> Deucalion, waiting for him with his arm weighed down by
> the spear, looked Death in the face. Achilles struck the man's
> neck with his sword and sent head and helmet flying off
> together. The marrow welled up from the vertebrae, and the
> corpse lay stretched on the ground. The next quarry of
> Achilles was Rhigmus, the noble son of Peiros, who had

come from the deep-soiled land of Thrace. He cast at him and caught him full. The bronze javelin came to rest in his lung and he tumbled from his chariot. . . . Thus Achilles ran amuck with his spear. . . . He chased his victims with the fury of a fiend, and the earth was dark with blood. At their imperious master's will the horses of Achilles with their massive hooves trampled dead men and shields alike with no more ado than when a farmer had yoked a pair of broad-browed cattle to trample the white barley on a threshing-floor and his lowing bulls tread out the grain. The axle-tree under his chariot, and the rails that ran round it, were sprayed with the blood thrown up by the horses' hooves and by the tyres. And the son of Peleus pressed on in search of glory, bespattering his unconquerable hands with gore. —XX, p. 378.

We get, in all this attention to the gory, anatomical details of the battlefield, a fleeting glimpse of an ideal that is not too far removed from savagery. In this glorification of the butchery of warfare as a means to personal fame we have an aspect of the Greek epic ideal which contrasts sharply with that of the Romans. But whether it was won by wily debate or by prowess on the battlefield, there is no possible doubt that personal glory was the dominant element in the primitive Greek heroic ideal, and for Achilles it was definitely glory won on the battlefield.

It is also important to notice that Achilles is not criticized in *The Iliad* for his stand in the matter of his personal honor. On the contrary, it is conceded by the gods and men alike that he had a genuine grievance and had a right to demand reparation from Agamemnon. In the first place, his goddess-mother, Thetis, is on his side from the beginning. Achilles asks her to persuade Zeus to help him get amends from Agamemnon:

"Persuade him [Zeus], if you can [he begs Thetis] to help the Trojans, to fling the Achaeans back on their ships, to pen them in against the sea and slaughter them. That would teach them to appreciate their King. That would make im-

perial Agamemnon son of Atreus realize what a fool he was
to insult the noblest of them all."—I, pp. 33-34.

Thetis uses her influence with Zeus and wins a promise from
him to espouse the cause of her injured son:

> "Father Zeus, [she pleads] . . . grant me a wish and
> show your favour to my son. He is already singled out for
> early death, and now Agamemnon king of men has affronted
> him. He has stolen his prize and kept her for himself. Avenge
> my son, Olympian Judge, and let the Trojans have the upper
> hand till the Achaeans pay him due respect and make him
> full amends."—I, p. 36.

Zeus agrees to let the Trojans have their day in order to humble
Agamemnon and exalt Achilles. "Zeus had in mind," we are
told in Book XIII, "victory for the Trojans and Hector, with
a view to exalting Achilles" (XIII, p. 243). Again when Zeus
assures her that the ultimate victory will go to the Achaeans, he
reminds her that for the present the Trojans will be victorious
to fulfill the wishes of Achilles:

> "But in the meantime, [he says] I remain hostile to the
> Danaans, and I will not permit any other of the immortals
> to come down to their assistance before the wishes of Achilles
> are fulfilled, in accordance with the promise I gave him (and
> confirmed with a nod of my head) that day when the divine
> Thetis put her arms around my knees and implored me to
> vindicate her son, the sacker of cities."—XV, p. 273.

This would certainly suggest that both Thetis and Zeus considered Achilles to be right. When the sea-god, Poseidon, is
trying to bestir the disheartened Achaeans to make a last-ditch
stand at the ships against the Trojans, he admits that Agamemnon is to blame for their sad straits by having insulted Achilles,
but he says nothing derogatory of Achilles himself. This is part
of his incendiary speech:

[25]

"Now, they [the Trojans] have left their city far behind them and are fighting by the hollow ships, all through the incompetence of our Commander-in-Chief and the slackness of the troops, who are so disgusted with their leader that they would rather die beside their fast ships than defend them. Yet even if the whole blame does rest with our overlord Agamemnon son of Atreus, who insulted the great runner Achilles, we have no excuse whatever for giving up the struggle."—XIII, pp. 236-237.

The gods, then, either take it for granted or positively state that Achilles was in the right and Agamemnon in the wrong, and they positively intervene to help Achilles achieve his end of humiliating Agamemnon and of bringing the whole Achaean host to recognize his own superiority over their king.

The attitude of the gods is echoed in that of practically all the important Achaean leaders. The first criticism of Agamemnon, however, comes by way of an ironic jest from the comedian Thersites. But what he says is not all jest. He accuses Agamemnon of practically all the capital sins—greed, lust, and cowardice, and then turns on the soldiery and calls them a crowd of women.

"As for you, my friends, poor specimens that you are, Achaean women—I cannot call you men—let us sail home by all means and leave this fellow [Agamemnon] here to fatten on his spoils and find out how completely he depends on the ranks. Why, only a little while ago he insulted Achilles, a far better man than he is. He walked off with his prize and kept her for himself. But it needs more than that to make Achilles lose his temper. He takes things lying down. Otherwise, my lord, that outrage would have been your last."—II, p. 46.

When we recall the towering rage of Achilles and the fact that if the gods had not intervened he would have killed Agamemnon on the spot, Thersites' description of Achilles as a restrained man is highly ironic. Although Thersites is cruelly cuffed into silence by Odysseus, both Odysseus and the other Achaean leaders recognize that there is much truth in what he has said and say so themselves on other occasions.

The first to criticize Agamemnon seriously is wise old Nestor. At a council meeting of all the Achaeans, he tells Agamemnon that he was utterly wrong in taking Briseis from Achilles.

> "We were all against it; [he says] and I, for one, did my utmost to dissuade you. But your arrogant temper got the better of you and you degraded a man of highest distinction, whom the gods themselves esteem, by confiscating his prize, to your own profit. Which brings me to my point. Even at this late hour let us take steps to approach and placate him with peace offerings and a humble apology."—IX, p. 164.

That leaves little doubt about where Nestor considers the rights to lie. When the revered old Phoenix is trying to persuade Achilles to rejoin the Achaeans he tells Achilles he is overly stubborn for not accepting the reparation that Agamemnon has offered to make to him. But there is no suggestion that Achilles is wrong in his fundamental attitude toward Agamemnon; on the contrary, Phoenix admits that "nobody can blame you for the resentment you have felt till now" (IX, p. 175). And Odysseus, in a speech which he makes to both Agamemnon and Achilles, when the latter has finally agreed to rejoin the battle, tells Agamemnon publicly to display all the gifts he has promised Achilles to advertise his willingness to make reparation to him, to return Briseis, and to swear before the whole Achaean host that he has never slept with her. All this to vindicate Achilles. Achilles is also advised to show a forgiving spirit. But the final advice goes to Agamemnon.

> "Then, as a peace offering, let him [Agamemnon] give you [Achilles] a rich banquet in his hut and so complete your vindication. And may I recommend *you*, my lord Atreides, to be more scrupulous in your future dealings? It is no disgrace

for a king, when he has given offence, to come forward and
repair the breach."—XIX, p. 358.

Odysseus, like all the rest, lays the burden of the blame on
Agamemnon. Agamemnon is never advised to forgive Achilles,
because fundamentally Achilles has done nothing for which
he needs forgiveness. Achilles has been right, and Agamemnon
has been wrong.

And what does Agamemnon say about all this himself?
He is the very first to admit that he was utterly unjustified in
his conduct toward Achilles. It is true that he explains his conduct by blaming the gods for entangling him in a coil of Ate,
but that still makes Achilles' resentment justifiable. In the very
first public council he admits to Nestor that in the quarrel with
Achilles he was the first to lose his temper (II, p. 50). And this
was his answer to Nestor's later advice that he make a humble
apology to Achilles:

> "My venerable lord, the account of my blind folly that
> you have given us is wholly true. Blinded I was—I do not
> deny it myself. The man whom Zeus has taken to his heart
> and honours as he does Achilles, to the point of crushing the
> Achaeans for his sake, is worth an army. But since I did give
> in to a lamentable impulse and commit this act of folly, I am
> willing to go back on it and propitiate him with a handsome
> indemnity."—IX, p. 164.

Although he throws more blame on the gods in doing so, Agamemnon later repeats all this and more to Achilles himself,
when the feud has ended and Achilles is girding himself to go
into battle once more.

> "The Achaeans have often cried out against me, making
> the very point with which you, sir, began your speech. But I
> was not to blame. It was Zeus and Fate and the Fury who
> walks in the dark that blinded my judgment, that day at the
> meeting, when on my own authority I confiscated Achilles'

prize. What could I do? At such moments there is a Power
that takes complete command, Ate, the eldest Daughter of
Zeus. . . . But since I *was* blinded and Zeus robbed me of my
wits, I am willing to make amends and pay you ample compensation."—XIX, pp. 356-357.

It is true that Achilles is criticized by several of the
Achaeans for his prolonged rancor, but nobody ever denies
that he has a grievance and the right to redress from Agamemnon. And almost without exception, these criticisms occur in
speeches in which the speakers are trying to persuade Achilles
to get back into the conflict and save the sorely pressed Achaeans. The speakers all try to show him that he is going too far
in hanging on to his grudge against Agamemnon when the
king has already admitted his fault and shown himself willing
to make full reparation; but all, like Phoenix, would admit
that "nobody can blame [him] for the resentment [he has]
felt till now." The old man Phoenix is the first to criticize
him;[15] Odysseus does so on at least one occasion,[16] Diomedes
is quite forthright in his criticism,[17] as is Ajax in his,[18] and
finally even his friend Patroclus on the advice of Nestor tells
him he has gone too far in nursing his grudge "warping a noble
nature to ignoble ends." [19] When Achilles finally does relent,
like Agamemnon, he blames his stubborn wrath on Ate, a blind
power that has possessed him; but, as we have seen, he never
denies that he was justified in his fundamental resentment
against Agamemnon for having so dishonored him in the eyes
of the Achaean host. The only mistake he ever admits to is
having harbored his indignation too long;[20] the indignation itself would to him and to his fellow Achaeans look more like
a virtue than a vice. Recall, again, old Phoenix' remark: "Nobody can blame you for the resentment you have felt till now."
The whole action of *The Iliad* was, as we have seen, arranged
to vindicate Achilles in his resentment.

It would seem, then, that a careful reading of *The Iliad*
justifies the conclusion that Achilles is a man whose supreme
value in life is his own personal honor and glory. He is a man

for whom the Greeks would have had more admiration than pity. Certainly they would have had for him little if any of the contempt that we feel for a proud and egotistical individual. Difficult as it may be for us in reading *The Iliad* to tolerate the arrogance of Achilles, we should try to remember that for the Greeks he, like Odysseus, would have been predominantly an epic hero whom they admired rather than a tragic one whom they pitied.

There is a sense, of course, in which Achilles may be said to be a pathetic figure. That, incidentally, is how Aristotle characterizes the whole *Iliad* in *The Poetics*, Chapter 24. It is, he says, παθητικόν, in contrast to the *Odyssey*, which is ήθικον. Lane Cooper translates παθητικόν as "tragic"; Butcher more correctly, it seems to me, translates it "pathetic." A pathetic situation for Aristotle is one that is not the outcome of human choice. What part of *The Iliad* answers to that description? In one sense the whole of it. Both the main characters claim that they are victims of the gods who have steered them into their actions and the resultant situations. Agamemnon claims it was Ate sent by the gods that induced his unjust treatment of Achilles in the first place:

> "The Achaeans have often cried out against me, making the very point with which you, sir, began your speech. But I was not to blame. It was Zeus and Fate and the Fury who walks in the dark that blinded my judgment, that day at the meeting, when on my own authority I confiscated Achilles' prize. What could I do? At such moments there is a Power that takes complete command, Ate, the eldest Daughter of Zeus, who blinds us all, accursed spirit that she is."—XIX, p. 356.

And Achilles, in turn, also blames his prolonged wrath on the gods. In a sense, then, both Agamemnon and Achilles are pathetic figures used as pawns in the hands of the gods for their larger designs. And there is still more pathos in the situation of Achilles particularly. We are constantly reminded that, great and successful though he is, he is destined to an early death on the plains of Troy. His mother, Thetis, is forever bewailing the fact and using it to win present favors from the gods for her son. Whether she is addressing the gods or Achilles himself, Thetis' theme is the same: "He is already singled out for early death" (I, p. 36); "You surely have not long to live; for after Hector's death you are doomed forthwith to die" (XVIII, p. 339); on one occasion we get a glimpse of Thetis "in her vaulted cavern, surrounded by a gathering of other salt-sea Nymphs, in whose midst she was bewailing the lot of her peerless son, destined as she knew to perish in the deep-soiled land of Troy far from his own country" (XXIV, p. 439). Achilles himself is also aware of his early doom and rings variations on the theme. To Thetis: "As for my death, when Zeus and the other deathless gods appoint it, let it come" (XVIII, p. 340). To old Priam: "Am I not big and beautiful, the son of a great man, with a goddess for my Mother? Yet Death and Sovran Destiny are waiting for me too. A morning is coming, or maybe an evening or noon, when somebody is going to kill me too in battle with a cast of the spear or an arrow from his bow" (XXI, p. 383). To the dead Patroclus: "Since I shall never see my country again, I propose to part with this lock [of his own hair which his father promised to offer up to Spercheus at Achilles' safe return home] and give it to my lord Patroclus" (XXIII, p. 416). Achilles was also reminded of his early doom by the ghost of Patroclus: "For I have been engulfed by the dreadful fate that must have been my lot at birth; and it is your destiny too, most worshipful Achilles, to perish under the walls of the rich town of Troy" (XXIII, p. 414). So much has this thought become a part of Achilles' own mental machinery that he says in his long speech to the suppliant Priam: "We men are wretched things, and the gods, who have no cares themselves, have woven sorrow into the very pattern of our lives" (XXIV, p. 451). It can rightly be said, then, that *The Iliad* is pathetic and that there is pathos in the character of Achilles; but that is by no means the same as saying that the work as a whole, much less the character of Achilles, is tragic. In the main action of the poem, that struggle of Achilles to humiliate Agamemnon and regain his own honored position in the eyes of the Achaean host, Achilles is only very mildly pathetic and not tragic at all. He is far more admired for the action he takes to stand up for his rights than pitied as a plaything of the gods. His life is the mixed kind of good fortune and ill that he describes in his parable to Priam, but we feel that he himself would estimate his own life as more fortunate than ill in spite of his doom of an early death. He had lived gloriously; he had fought gloriously; he died gloriously and was gloriously honored after death; and he had the assurance that his glorious reputation would live on in the ears of men forever. What more could a Greek hero want?

NOTES

[1] The most recent critic to have advanced the view that *The Iliad* is a tragic story is L. A. Post in *From Homer to Menander* (Berkeley: University of California Press, 1951). The entire chapter entitled "The Tragic Pattern of the *Iliad*" develops this point of view; the following is perhaps the clearest statement of it; "Achilles' tragedy is the loss of his illusions. He had lost his honor in surviving Patroclus. That to him was worse than death, and no reconciliation of his quarrel with his fate was now possible. Whether or not the future is determined, the past is certainly irrevocable. The tragedy of Achilles was complete in Book 18 of the *Iliad* when he learned of the death of Patroclus. He might have fought beside his friend, but had not done so because he was thinking of glory and honor and would not fight before Agamemnon had apologized. His pride was his downfall, and the greater blow to his pride, when his friend was lost, was his tragedy" (p. 47). C. M. Bowra, in *Tradition and Design in the Iliad* (Oxford: The Clarendon Press, 1930) like many other Homeric critics, also insists on the tragic character of *The Iliad*. "The story of the wrath of Achilles, as the poet announces it, is thus the kernel of the *Iliad*. It is a tragic story in so far as it involves waste and loss or excites pity and fear. And the tragedy is essentially moral. It turns on the fail-

ure of Achilles to keep his αἰδώς for gods and men, and it does not end till he has regained it. This failure is due to his imperious temper, and is thus derived from the same source as his heroic qualities in war and council. His great gifts have their tragic side and lead to the death of Patroclus and his own humiliation" (p. 22). See also *ibid.*, pp. 23-25. It is my contention that Homer does not intend us to pity Achilles in the central action of the story; nor does he represent him as being pitied by his fellow Achaeans. As we shall see, they rather admired him for having the courage to stand up for his *rights* of honor from Agamemnon. It is not Achilles who is humiliated by the action of the poem but rather Agamemnon at the hands of Achilles. The poem ends with Achilles triumphant; he has gained all that he set out to get—a redress from Agamemnons' slight. In this he is admired. He may be pitied for his fated early death, but that too he preferred to a return home without honor.

2 In his *Poetics*, Aristotle describes *The Iliad* as pathetic rather than tragic. See the final paragraph of this chapter for a discussion of this point.

3 Achilles states on several occasions that this is the unforgivable insult. Thus he says to Patroclus when the latter is trying to persuade him to rejoin the battle: "What has cut me to the quick is that a fellow no better than myself should want to plunder me and take away the prize I won, just because he has more power. After all I have gone through in the war, it is more than I can bear. That girl—the army made a special point of giving her to me; I had sacked a walled town; I had won her with my own spear. And now she is snatched from my arms by King Agamemnon son of Atreus, and I am served like a disreputable tramp."—*Iliad*, XVI, p. 293. See also IX, p. 170. Page references here and in quotations from *The Iliad* throughout are to the translation by F. V. Rieu, in the Penguin Classics, and are reprinted by permission of Penguin Books Ltd. When quotations from the text of *The Iliad* are cited in the text itself, reference to the book of *The Iliad* and to the pages of this translation will be given immediately after the quotation.

4 He volunteers to accept Hector's challenge to single combat (VII, p. 134), but is dissuaded from doing so by Agamemnon who tells him "not to let ambition make [him] fight a better man." "Even Achilles," Agamemnon reminds him, "feared to meet him

in the field of honour, and Achilles is a better man than you by far." But Menelaus is definitely not the man who deems honor the highest good (and in this he is sharply contrasted with Achilles). When he is endeavoring to recover the body of Patroclus and is threatened by Hector he muses thus with himself: "If I abandon these fine arms and the body of Patroclus, who fell here fighting to exact repayment for my wrongs, I shall be an object of contempt to any Danaan who sees me. But if for honour's sake I fight with Hector and the Trojans single-handed, I am likely to be cut off and overwhelmed, for Hector of the bright helmet has all the Trojans at his heels" (XVII, p. 318). He abandons the body, justifying his doing so by telling himself that it is foolish to fight against what has been fated by the gods.

⁵ In many ways Hector seems to the modern reader a much more admirable character than Achilles himself. His cause in general is much less self-centered than that of Achilles; he is fighting, after all, for the protection of his city, his parents, and his family. And the scenes in which he, Andromache, and his baby boy, Astyanax, figure are some of the most humanly touching in all of literature. But it is worth noticing here that even the noble Hector is not unaffected by the notion of Aristotelian honor. Thus in the farewell speech he makes to Andromache, he reminds her that he could not think of shirking battle "for I have trained myself always, like a good soldier, to take my place in the front line and win glory for my father and myself" (VI, p. 129). When he challenges the Greeks to single combat he assures them that if he kills the challenger he will send back his body to them that they may build a proper monument for it so that strangers, seeing it, will say: " 'This is the monument of some warrior of an earlier day who was killed in single combat by illustrious Hector!' Thus my fame will be kept alive forever" (VII, p. 134). When he has risked the whole Trojan army by refusing to follow the advice of Polydamas to retreat before Achilles within the walls, he finally sizes up his desperate situation in these words: "If I retire behind the gate and wall, Polydamas will be the first to cast it in my teeth that, in this last night of disaster when the great Achilles came to life, I did not take his advice and order a withdrawal into the city, as I certainly ought to have done. As it is, having sacrificed the army to my perversity, I could not face my countrymen and the Trojan

ladies in their trailing gowns. I could not bear to hear some commoner say: 'Hector trusted in his own right arm and lost an army.'
But it *will* be said, and then I shall know that it would have been a
far better thing for me to stand up to Achilles, and either kill him
and come home alive or myself die gloriously in front of Troy"
(XXII, pp. 399-400). Here at the crucial point in Hector's life, it
is not the best interests of his army nor of his city or family that
decide the issue, but his own personal glory. In the very heat of
battle wtih Achilles, too, this is still a prominent thought with him.
This is his prayer as he hurls his spear at Achilles: "So now I meet
my doom. Let me at least sell my life dearly and have a not inglorious end, after some feat of arms that shall come to the ears of generations still unborn" (XXII, p. 405). Finally, Andromache shows
herself aware of this trait in her husband. When she has a premonition of his death, she says of him: "Hector would never hang
back with the crowd; he always sallied out in front of all the rest
and let no one be as daring as himself" (XXII, p. 409).

⁶ This is the greeting he gives Ajax and Odysseus when they
come from Agamemnon to try to persuade him to rejoin the battle:
"Heralds, ambassadors of Zeus and men, I welcome you. Come forward. My quarrel is not with you but with Agamemnon, who sent
you here to fetch the girl Briseis" (I, p. 32). And on their second
visit: "Welcome—to two dear friends! It was time that someone
came; and angry as I am, there are no two Achaeans whom I love
more than you" (IX, p. 166).

⁷ Recall that Aristotle says that the magnanimous man is
haughty "towards people who enjoy high position and good fortune, but unassuming towards those of the middle class; for it is
a difficult and lofty thing to be superior to the former, but easy to
be so to the latter, and a lofty bearing over the former is no mark
of ill-breeding, but among humble people it is as vulgar as a display
of strength against the weak."—*Nic. Ethics*, 1124b-15. This would
explain Achilles' hauteur and even insolence toward Agamemnon
and his kindness and condescension toward Ajax and Odysseus and
other lesser Achaeans. Aristotle also says that the magnanimous
man is "not an evil-speaker, even about his enemies, except from
haughtiness" (1125a-5). It was to manifest his own superiority over
and his contempt for Agamemnon that Achilles flung all his insolent speeches at him. Recall especially the speeches in Book I.

⁸ *Nic. Ethics*, 1125a-1.

⁹ Achilles frequently assumes a stoic attitude toward his death. About death itself he can be indifferent, but not about the circumstances that are to surround it. This is his worry when death threatens him in his struggle with the River Scamander. "Ah, why could Hector not have killed me? He is the finest man they have bred in Troy, and the killer would have been as noble as the killed. But now it seems that I was doomed to die a villainous death, caught in a great river, like a boy in charge of the pigs who is swept away by a mountain stream that he has tried to cross in spate" (XXI, p. 387). It is not death that is his worry, but the lack of glory that may surround it.

¹⁰ When Agamemnon volunteers for the spear-throwing contest against Meriones, he is put off with this gracious gesture by Achilles: "My Lord Atreides, we know by how much you excell the rest of us, and that in throwing the spear no one can compete with your prowess. Accept this prize [an unused cauldron] and take it with you to the hollow ships. But if you are agreeable, let us give the spear to my lord Meriones. That is what I at all events suggest. To this decision, Agamemnon King of Men made no demur" (XXIII, p. 436). Agamemnon had evidently learned his lesson and was making no more demur where Achilles was involved.

¹¹ The translation of *The Odyssey* referred to throughout this section is that by E. V. Rieu, in the Penguin Classics, and is reprinted by permission of Penguin Books, Ltd.

¹² *Iliad*, IX, p. 172. Achilles had phrased that alternative himself in these words: "Thetis of the Silver Feet, says that Destiny has left two courses open to me on my journey to the grave. If I stay here and play my part in the siege of Troy, there is no homecoming for me, though I shall win undying fame. But if I go home to my own country, my good name will be lost, though I shall have long life, and shall be spared an early death."

¹³ The Romans were understandably rather unsympathetic with the Greek heroic ideal. They oversimplified it into a composite of force and fraud. For them Achilles embodied the former and Odysseus the latter. Of the two they despised the fraudulent Odysseus the more. Even a cursory reading of *The Odyssey* convinces one that the cleverness developed even to the point of trickery and deceit which characterized Odysseus' every action was

much admired by the Greeks. They delighted in his wiliness as a sign of his superior intelligence. It is that quality that gives consistency to the character of Odysseus and unity to the variety of episodes in *The Odyssey*. The goddess Athena, of considerable resourcefulness herself, admires him for his wilines and co-operates with him in several guileful adventures. Her attitude toward him as he warily accepts the news from her that he is at home in Ithaca at last expresses the whole Greek attitude toward this human trait. "What a cunning knave it would take," she said, "to beat you at your tricks! Even a god would be hard put to it. And so my stubborn friend, Odysseus, the arch-deceiver, with his craving for intrigue, does not propose even in his own country to drop his sharp practice and lying tales that he loves from the bottom of his heart. But no more of this: we are both adepts in chicane. For in the world of men you have no rival as statesman and orator, while I am pre-eminent among the gods for invention and resource."— *Odyssey*, XIII, pp. 209-210. In the war of Troy, Odysseus had become famous for devising the scheme of the Trojan horse; in his wanderings after the war, he had talked and tricked his way out of one difficulty after another; and once back in Ithaca, his whole energies were devoted to the intrigue with Telemachus and the faithful servants for the undoing of the suitors. From the moment he landed in Ithaca, he positively reveled in one tall tale after another about his past exploits. It is interesting to compare the tales he tells (in quick succession) about his identity and wanderings to Athena, to the shepherd Eumaeus, to the swineherd Antinous, to the suitor Amphinomus, to Penelope, and finally to his father Laertes. They are all completely different and all cut out of completely new cloth. But the point in all this to be emphasized here is that the Greeks admired Odysseus immensely for his achievements in this line. πολύμητις or πολυμήχανος, Odysseus of many wiles —these were laudatory and by no means critical epithets on Greek lips. How different the story and how different the epithets when we hear them on the lips of Virgil in *Aeneid*, II. A recent study by W. B. Stanford, *The Ulysses Theme* (Oxford: Basil Blackwell, 1954), points out, however, that Odysseus is not the typical Greek hero. That appellation is given to the more self-centered Achilles. See the chapter entitled "The Untypical Hero," pp. 66-81.

[37]

[14] *Nic. Ethics*, 1124b-7.

[15] See *Iliad*, IX, pp. 174-175, for Phoenix' long, persuasive speech to induce Achilles to join the battle again. In it he says: "Conquer your pride, Achilles, you have no right to be so stubborn. The very gods, for all their greater excellence and majesty and power are capable of being swayed. Even they are turned from their course by sacrifice and humble prayers. . . . If my Lord Agamemnon had not made you a generous offer, with the promise of more to come, but had persisted in his rancour, I should be the last person to bid you cast your anger to the winds and help the Argives, however great their need. But as it is, he is not only offering you a great deal now, but has pledged himself to future liberality, besides choosing as ambassadors to plead his cause the most distinguished men in the whole army, who are your own best friends amongst the Argives. Their pleas, their pilgrimage here, are things that you must not dismiss as trifles, though nobody can blame you for the resentment you have felt till now."

[16] Odysseus, in one of his speeches, reminds Achilles of the parting caution of his father Peleus when he sent him on the expedition to Troy. "My good friend, when your father Peleus sent you from Phthia to join Agamemnon, did he not admonish you in these words: 'My son, Athene and Here, if they wish you well, are going to make you strong. What *you* must do is to keep a check on that proud spirit of yours; for a kind heart is a better thing than pride. Quarrels are deadly. Be reconciled at once; and all the Argives young and old will look up to you the more'? Those were the old man's precepts—which you have forgotten. Yet even so it is not too late for you to yield" (IX, pp. 167-168).

[17] This is Diomedes' comment to Agamemnon on the news of Achilles' refusal to rejoin the battle: "It is a thousand pities that you brought yourself to plead with my lord Achilles and make him such a princely offer. He is a proud man at the best of times; and now you have given him an even better conceit of himself" (IX, p. 179).

[18] Ajax remarks to Odysseus, when their mission to Achilles has been fruitless: "I cannot help reflecting on the combination of rancour and arrogance that Achilles has displayed. Ruthlessness too. Not a thought for the affection of his comrades, who made him the idol of our camp" (IX, pp. 177-178).

[38]

[19] Patroclus, in the speech which finally persuades Achilles to allow him to go into battle to save the Achaean ships, among other things, says this to Achilles: "Heaven preserve me from the vindictive feelings you cherish, warping a noble nature to ignoble ends. What will future generations have to thank you for, if you will not help the Argives in their direst needs? Pitiless man, you are no son of Thetis and the gallant Peleus. Only the gray sea and its frowning crags could have produced a monster so hard-hearted" (XVI, pp. 292-93). These are harsh words, and they finally break through the stubbornness of Achilles. He repeats his complaint: "What has cut me to the quick is that a fellow no better than myself should want to plunder me and take away the prize I won, just because he has more power. After all I have gone through in the war, it is more than I can bear." But he finally relents: "What is done cannot be undone. I was wrong in supposing that a man could nurse a grudge forever, though I did think of keeping up the feud till the tumult and the fighting reached my own ships" (XVI, p. 293). Notice Achilles does not withdraw what he considers his just complaint against Agamemnon, but admits only he was wrong in keeping up the feud too long. And that is all his critics have criticized him for. Witness, too, the fact that not even Patroclus would criticize Achilles' fundamental attitude toward Agamemnon in the speech he makes to the soldiers before he leads them off to battle: "Myrmidons, soldiers of Prince Achilles, be men, my friends, display your old audacity, and win glory for the son of Peleus, the best man in the Argive camp with the best companies in his command. Teach his imperial majesty King Agamemnon what a fool he was when he trifled with the best Achaean of them all" (XVI, p. 299). This should make it clear enough that Patroclus' criticism of Achilles is not for his stand against Agamemnon—that is justified—but rather for his taking it out on the whole Achaean army.

[20] See note 19.

CHAPTER THREE

Cicero's Magnanimous Man

"It is our duty, then, to be more ready to endanger our own than the public welfare and to hazard honour and glory more readily than other advantages."
CICERO: *De Officiis*, I, xxiv

In contrast to the self-absorption and exaggerated concern for personal fame that prevail in Aristotle's discussion of the great-souled man, it is duty that is the focus of attention in Roman descriptions of him. The importance of duty had, of course, been emphasized by the Greek Stoics, but Stoicism can hardly be said to be the most characteristic of the many Greek philosophic attitudes. And even the Stoic sage was notorious for his individualism and aloofness from the social scene. But in Rome a modified Stoicism became the most widely accepted philosophy. Its emphasis on the all importance of moral earnestness and duty fitted in with the more practical and social-minded Roman temperament. In the Roman ideal it was not the personal glory of the individual Roman that was to the fore but rather the glory of the State. It was not Caesar so much as Rome that was the focus of attention; even Caesar deified was less a god than a symbol of Rome and the Empire. The Roman ideal was always social rather than individualistic. Perhaps that is one reason why there *was* a Roman Empire, whereas Greece politically never attained to anything beyond separate city-states forever jealous of and warring on one another.

If Aristotle has given us the most characteristic definition of the Greek ideal man, Cicero has, perhaps, best sketched the Roman ideal. In many ways Cicero himself is typical of the whole of Roman culture. He is derivative, more interested in the practical than the speculative; and he is eclectic in his views but, in his eclecticism, inclines more to Stoicism than to any other one system of thought. His discussion of the magnanimous man, then, may be taken as a fairly typical expression of Roman thought on the matter. He actually composed a whole treatise on the subject of glory, but unfortunately it has been lost. He says enough about it in his *De Officiis*,[1] however, to give us a sufficiently clear notion of his ideas on the subject.

The very title of this work "On Duties" suggests the whole Roman bent in the matter of human greatness. Glory or honor is still an important reality, but it is no longer the almost exclusive interest and supreme good that it was for the Greeks. With Cicero and the Romans in general we are breathing quite a different atmosphere from that created by Aristotle. The Roman ideal is closer to that of Plato in *The Republic* than to that of Aristotle in the *Nicomachean Ethics*.[2] Cicero takes it as much for granted as does Aristotle that the great-souled man deserves the highest honor, but he does not make personal glory the end-all and be-all of life. He insists, in fact, that self-interest is not the supreme good (I, ii, p. 5). There are times when one's own glory and reputation have to be sacrificed to a higher good, to the good of the commonweal.

> It is our duty, then, to be more ready to endanger our own than the public welfare and to hazard honour and glory more readily than other advantages.
>
> Many, on the other hand, have been found who were ready to pour out not only their money but their lives for their country and yet would not consent to make even the slightest sacrifice of personal glory—even though the interests of their country demanded it.—I, xxiv, 83-84.

[41]

This is an attitude quite different from that of the Aristotelian hero who is ready to sacrifice everything, even life itself, to the preservation of his own personal honor and glory.

The basis of honor for Cicero, as for Aristotle, is pre-eminence in virtue or moral goodness. "That moral goodness which we look for in a lofty, high-minded spirit is secured, of course, by moral not by physical strength," he says in one place (I, xxiii, 79). But, unlike Aristotle, Cicero emphasizes the virtues which are social in character rather than those qualities that focus attention on the excellence of the individual in himself. In discussing the marks of true fortitude he summarizes what for him are the two most important qualities of the truly great man:

> The soul that is altogether courageous and great is marked above all by two characteristics; one of these is indifference to outward circumstances; for such a person cherishes the conviction that nothing but moral goodness and propriety deserves to be either admired or wished for or striven after, and that he ought not to be subject to any man or any passion or any accident of fortune. The second characteristic is that, when the soul is disciplined in the way above mentioned, one should do deeds not only great and in the highest degree useful, but extremely arduous and laborious and fraught with danger both to life and to many things that make life worth living.—I, xx, 66.

What is to be noted here is the emphasis on moral goodness as the foundation of any true human greatness, but, even more important, the insistence on the necessity of the truly great man's doing great deeds useful to others even at the cost of a great deal of sacrifice to his own interests. Cicero's great man is not to find his happiness in retirement, where he preens himself on his own intellectual and moral excellence, but in a career in which he can devote these virtues to the commonweal. His greatest honor will be derived from such public-minded activity.[3]

Aristotle's great man, we recall, was never to allow his life to revolve around any other man; he was always to maintain his proper independence and aloofness. The chief glory of Cicero's great man, in contrast, arises from his fulfillment of his duties to others. Cicero reiterates again and again that it is the *just* dealings of the great man in his public career that form the surest basis for his esteem by the many. "If anyone wishes to win true glory, let him discharge the duties required by justice" (II, xiii, 43). Justice is pre-eminently a social virtue; and justice, for Cicero, "is the crowning glory of the virtues and on the basis of [it] men are called 'good men'; and, close akin to justice, charity, which may also be called kindness or generosity" (I, vii, 20). If these remarks leave any doubt about the social tone of Cicero's ideal, the following passage will put it beyond the shadow of doubt:

> But since, as Plato has admirably expressed it, we are not born for ourselves alone, but our country claims a share of our being, and our friends a share; and since, as the Stoics hold, everything that the earth produces is created for man's use; and as men, too, are born for the sake of men, that they may be able mutually to help one another; in this direction we ought to follow Nature as our guide, to contribute to the general good by an interchange of acts of kindness, by giving and receiving, and thus by our skill, our industry, and our talents to cement human society more closely together, man to man.—I, vii, 22.

For Cicero, the only difference between the great-souled man and his fellow men, in this respect, is that the great-souled man, by reason of his greater talents, has more to contribute to the commonweal, and consequently a more solemn duty to contribute it. So much is the social aspect of the ideal emphasized here and elsewhere that it begins to savor of the aberration of the rather complete subordination of the individual to the state—the direct opposite of the characteristic Greek aberration.

In Book II of the *De Officiis,* where Cicero pauses to analyze the means of enhancing one's reputation or glory with the populace, it is again apparent that the chief bases for esteem are the services done to the commonweal.

> Good-will is won principally through kind services; next to that, it is elicited by the will to do a kind service, even though nothing happen to come of it. Then, too, the love of people generally is powerfully attracted by a man's mere name and reputation for generosity, kindness, justice, honour, and all those virtues that belong to gentleness of character and affability of manner.—II, ix, 32.

How completely foreign this is to the self-satisfaction, haughtiness, and indifference to the esteem of inferiors that are recorded as virtues of the Aristotelian hero.

This exalted social-minded ideal of Cicero was, of course, not very often achieved by Romans in public life. The danger to the greatly gifted leader always is that he become self-willed and tyrannical, and Cicero was very much aware of that danger.

> The mischief is that from this exaltation and greatness of spirit spring all too readily self-will and excessive lust for power. . . . The more notable a man is for his greatness of spirit, the more ambitious he is to be the foremost citizen, or, I should say rather, to be sole ruler. But when one begins to aspire to pre-eminence, it is difficult to preserve that spirit of fairness which is absolutely essential to justice. The result is that such men do not allow themselves to be constrained either by argument or by any public and lawful authority; but they only too often prove to be bribers and agitators in public life, seeking to obtain supreme power and to be superiors through force rather than equals through justice. But the greater the difficulty, the greater the glory; for no occasion arises that can excuse a man for being guilty of injustice.—I, xix, 64.

But the point which is worthy of note here is that the ideal, for Cicero, is the great-souled man who dedicates his talent in justice to the service of his fellow men. And even Roman tyrants seemed to try to strengthen their positions by a reputation for justice and generosity, even if it were achieved only through a program of *panis et circenses*.

We have seen that Aristotle's hero sought the esteem of the great but was contemptuous of the opinion of his inferiors. His relationships with all his fellow mortals were self-centered. Cicero's great-souled man, on the contrary, is conscious of a whole hierarchy of fellow human beings to whom he is bound by bonds of duty. As a matter of fact, Cicero states that all men are bound to one another by like ties, but that the bond of duty binds the truly eminent man most of all. In the first place he is bound to all other human beings by the mere fact that they *are* human beings and not beasts.

> The first principle is that which is found in the connection subsisting between all the members of the human race; and that bond of connection is reason and speech, which by the processes of teaching and learning, of communicating, discussing, and reasoning associate men together and unite them in a sort of natural fraternity. . . . This, then, is the most comprehensive bond that unites together men as men, and all to all.—I, xvi, 50-51.

After discussing the closer bonds of union established by common citizenship, kinship, friendship, and love of country (I, xvii, 53-57), he goes on to state the degree of closeness established by these several bonds in a descending order of importance.

> If a contrast and comparison were to be made to find out where most of our moral obligation is due, country should come first, and parents; for their services have laid us under the heaviest obligations; next come children and the whole family, who look to us alone for support and can have no

other protection; finally, our kinsmen, with whom we live on good terms and with whom, for the most part, our lot is one.—I, xvii, 58.

In spite of the great stress laid on duty to the members of one's own family, and the great emphasis put on the bond of true friendship,[4] Cicero, in true Roman fashion, makes clear in this passage and the one that follows that the closest bond of all is that which exists between the citizen and his country.

But when with a rational spirit you have surveyed the whole field, there is no social relation among them all more close, none more dear than that which links each one of us with our country. Parents are dear; dear are children, relatives, friends; but one native land embraces all our loves; and who that is true would hesitate to give his life for her, if by his death he could render her a service?—I, xvii, 57.

It is worth noting that the emphasis here is again upon duty and service rather than upon the personal glory accruing from the performance of that duty and the rendering of that service.

In these passages Cicero is discussing the hierarchy of duties toward one's fellow men. He would not have been a Roman if he had not admitted that duty to the gods was higher than any of these social obligations. In another passage he concedes that, when he includes duty to the gods in his hierarchy:

Our first duty is to the immortal gods; our second to country; our third to parents; and so on, in a descending scale, to the rest.—I, xlv, 160.

This is only one among many statements by Cicero which emphasizes the sense of duty and service that should characterize the truly magnanimous man.

In light of the haughtiness and superior bearing which were to be the required mien of Aristotle's great-souled man,

it is interesting to hear Cicero cautioning those in public trusts
to avoid arrogance and pride and to be courteous and forbear-
ing in all their dealings with the public:

> Neither must we listen to those who think that one
> should indulge in violent anger against one's political ene-
> mies and imagine that such is the attitude of a great-spirited,
> brave man. For nothing is more commendable, nothing more
> becoming in a pre-eminently great man than courtesy and
> forbearance. . . . If punishment or correction must be admin-
> istered, it need not be insulting; it ought to have regard to the
> welfare of the state, not to the personal satisfaction of the
> man who administers the punishment or reproof.—I, xxv, 88.
>
> Again when fortune smiles and the stream of life flows
> according to our wishes, let us diligently avoid all arrogance,
> haughtiness, and pride. For it is as much a sign of weakness
> to give way to one's feelings in success as it is in adversity.
> —I, xxvi, 90.

One of the ways in which Aristotle's magnanimous man was to
manifest his great spirit was to show by mien and word his
anger with and contempt for a criticism leveled at him by an
equal. And so little did such wrath and haughty rejoinder seem
censurable to the Greeks that, as we have seen, they made the
wrath of Achilles the central theme of their greatest epic.

In Cicero's discussion of war, he again throws the emphasis on its social implications. In primitive heroic ideals, glory
won on the battlefield was almost the only glory that counted.
Aristotle had considerably moderated his hero's enthusiasm for
war; but we have seen that his magnanimous man was ready
enough to fight in a situation that was a challenge to his superior mettle because such a battle would redound to his own
glory. To Cicero war itself seems hateful:

> The only excuse . . . for going to war is that we may live
> in peace unharmed; and when the victory is won, we should
> spare those who have not been blood-thirsty and barbarous
> in their warfare.—I, xi, 35.

And even more striking is the following statement:

> Most people think that the achievements of war are more important than those of peace; but this opinion needs to be corrected. For many men have sought occasions for war from the mere ambition for fame. This is notably the case with men of great spirit and natural ability, and it is the more likely to happen, if they are adapted to a soldier's life and fond of warfare. But if we will face the facts, we shall find that there have been many instances of achievement in peace more important and no less renowned than in war.—I, xxii, 74.[5]

The most fundamental quality of all in the Greek hero was his intellectual acumen. The great stress on intelligence in all of Greek culture should make us expect that. Aristotle does not insist on the point in his definition of the magnanimous man, but rather takes it for granted. So highly regarded was intellectual sharpness by the Greeks that they considered it an admirable thing for their heroes to use trickery and deceit to gain their ends. In fact, this attitude prevailed so widely among the Greeks that the Romans came to think that all Greeks were liars.[6] For the Romans, who put so much emphasis on social equity,[7] such deceit was hateful, and many of them said so. In a famous passage of the *De Officiis*, Cicero condemns both force and fraud as means of gaining one's end.

> While wrong may be done, then, in either of two ways, that is, by force or by fraud, both are bestial: fraud seems to belong to the cunning fox, force to the lion; both are wholly unworthy of man, but fraud is the more contemptible.—I, xiii, 41.

Cicero is characteristically Roman here in considering deceit more hateful than force.

From all this, then, we would seem to be justified in saying that, for Cicero, the chief basis of honor for his great-spirited man was the willingness to sacrifice himself for the common-weal. In war or in peace, in good fortune or ill, he would be honored if it was apparent that he had fulfilled his duties to the commonweal. Duty to the gods, to the state, to the family, and to friends was to be the guiding star of a great Roman's life. So much was duty emphasized that the *rights* of the individual were sometimes lost sight of. The Roman was the exact opposite of the Greek situation where the "rights" of the individual were so exaggerated that clear *duties* to the state and one's fellow men were sometimes ignored.

NOTES

[1] CICERO: *De Officiis*. The selections used are reprinted by permission of the publishers and the Loeb Classical Library from Walter Miller (translator) (Cambridge, Mass., Harvard University Press, 1951). This edition has been used throughout this section. When quotations are cited in the text, the book, part, and page of this text will follow the quotation. When the exact text is not cited, the reference will also be given.

[2] It can be conceded that Roman practice seldom approached the ideal of social consciousness that Cicero depicts in the *De Officiis*, but the point is that his ideal *was* social-minded, whereas Aristotle's ideal man was selfish and almost antisocial.

[3] "The life of retirement is easier and safer and at the same time less burdensome or troublesome to others, while the career of those who apply themselves to statecraft and to conducting great enterprises is more profitable to mankind and contributes more to their own greatness and renown" (I, xxi, 70).

[4] It is worth citing here what Cicero says about the bond of friendship because it contrasts so sharply with the self-centeredness that pervades Aristotle's discussion of even that relationship: "But of all the bonds of fellowship, there is none more noble, none more powerful than when good men of congenial character are joined in intimate friendship; for really, if we discover in another that moral goodness on which I dwell so much, it attracts us and makes us friends to the one in whose character it seems to dwell. And while every virtue attracts us and makes us love those who seem

to possess it, still *justice* and *generosity* do most of all. Nothing, moreover, is more conducive to love and intimacy than compatability of character in good men. . . . Another strong bond of fellowship is effected by *mutual interchange of kind services;* and as long as these kindnesses are *mutual* and acceptable, those between whom they are interchanged are united by the ties of an enduring intimacy" (I, xvii, 55-56). Italics mine.

[5] The following statement, made a little later in the same book, also emphasizes Cicero's subordination of warlike exploits to those of peace: "And so diplomacy in the friendly settlement of controversies is more desirable than courage in settling them on the battlefield; but we must be careful not to take that course merely for the sake of avoiding war rather than for the sake of public expediency. War, however, should be undertaken in such a way as to make it evident that it has no other object than to secure peace" (I, xxiii, 80).

[6] Recall Virgil's comment relative to the Trojan horse, the eternal symbol for Romans of Greek deceit: "Timeo Danaos etiam dona ferentes." So little did the Greeks consider trickery and clever lying a vice that they elevated Odysseus, the cleverest Greek trickster and liar of them all, into the hero of one of their great epics. In *The Odyssey* we have the opportunity of watching him trick himself out of one situation after another. Even Plato granted his governors and philosopher-king the *privilege* of lying to the populace to get them to do things that were for their greater good. See *The Republic,* translated by Francis M. Cornford (New York: Oxford University Press, 1950), p. 78.

[7] Cicero, in contrast to the Greek attitude, is explicit in making practical, social-minded pursuits prior in their claims to merely speculative ones: "From all this we conclude that the duties prescribed by justice must be given precedence over the pursuit of knowledge and the duties imposed by it; for the former concern the welfare of our fellow-men; and nothing ought to be more sacred in men's eyes than that" (I, xliii, 155).

CHAPTER FOUR

Dutiful Aeneas,
the Typical Roman Hero

*"Be thy charge, O Roman, to rule the nations in
thine empire; this shall be thine art, to ordain the
law of peace, to be merciful to the conquered and
beat the haughty down."* VIRGIL: *Aeneid*, VI

Pius Aeneas—The very epithet which Virgil gives his hero sets
him apart from Achilles and distinguishes him as ideally Roman.
If, as Cicero tells us,[1] it was not personal glory but devotion
to duty that marked the true Roman, then Aeneas is unquestionably the truest Roman of them all. From first to last, duty
is the great driving force in his career and the final motive of
all his actions. His actions, in fact, exemplify the whole hierarchy of Roman duties as Cicero defines them—duty to the
gods, to the state, and to the family. *Pius Aeneas*, might, then,
best be translated as dutiful Aeneas.

From the very outset of *The Aeneid*, we are given to
understand that the story revolves around the duty of Aeneas
to found a new Troy, cost what it may to Aeneas personally
in wanderings and war.

I sing of arms and the man who came of old, a fated
wanderer, from the coasts of Troy to Italy and the shore of
Lavinium; hard driven on land and on the deep by the violence of heaven, by reason of cruel Juno's unforgetful anger,

[51]

and hard bestead in war also, ere he might found a city and carry his gods into Latium; from whom is the Latin race, the lords of Alba, and high-embattled Rome.—I, p. 1.[2]

We feel at once that here we are dealing with something far broader than a man's mere personal honor. This is the story of the fated wanderings and warfare of one man which are inextricably woven into the destinies of whole cities and peoples and of a whole empire. Aeneas himself may occasionally allow his great destiny to grow dim in his own mind; the endless wanderings and grim warfare may at times appear to him to be too great a price to pay for the founding of the new Troy; but, as the wanderings continue and the battles multiply, the reader is never allowed to forget that that is Aeneas' duty and final destiny. *Tantae molis erat Romanam condere gentem.* Such a task was it to found the Roman people (I, p. 2).

But great as was the task, Aeneas is represented by Virgil as capable of performing it. Virgil took him over as he found him in Homer. He was pictured there[3] as second only to Hector among the Trojans, a truly noble and courageous man. He had spirit enough to volunteer to take on Achilles himself in single combat, and would have done so had he not been restrained by Poseidon, who pointed out the foolhardiness of his trying to match the surpassing might and prowess of the great Greek hero. Like Achilles, Aeneas was himself half divine, since the goddess Venus was his mother; and Virgil occasionally allowed that divinity to shine through. Thus at his first appearance at the court of Dido he was "discovered in sheen of brilliant light, like a god in face and shoulders" (I, p. 18). Although Homer had made him no match for Achilles, he did picture him as a genuinely courageous man. For Virgil, of course, he was the paragon of bravery. He was not fond of warfare; but, when there was no other means to peace, no one could surpass him in battle. He took his place with the best of the Trojans in their last stand against the Greeks amid the burning ruins of Troy, and he withdrew from the desperate struggle only at the command of the gods. "I shunned no weapon or encounter," he himself says in his narrative to Dido, "and earned my fall at a Grecian hand, had destiny been thus" (II, p. 37). Aeneas was definitely no coward. But it is not chiefly for his prowess in battle but for his devotion to duty, and his general goodness that he is praised by his followers when they describe him to Dido.

> Aeneas was our king, foremost of men in righteousness, incomparable in goodness as in warlike arms.—I, p. 17.

As we shall see, these were also Aeneas' own values. War to him was a hateful thing in which he would acquit himself bravely if it was necessary, but he rather looked to be honored for the fulfillment of his duties to the gods, to the state, and to the family.

Although Aeneas was intended by Virgil to represent the virtuous Roman, it is well to note from the beginning, as Professor Bowra has pointed out,[4] that he represents virtue as the Stoics rather than as Aristotle conceived it. For Aristotle only the man who loved doing good was actually virtuous. If a man found it difficult to be temperate, for instance, but was temperate in spite of the difficulties, he would not be a virtuous man at all for Aristotle. For the Stoic, on the contrary, the virtuous life was thought of as very definitely a difficult thing, a warfare, in fact, beset by many hardships and temptations. The virtuous man's right to respect, for the Stoics, was not that he found it pleasant to be good, but rather that he was good in spite of the many difficulties that beset him on the path of goodness. This is definitely the atmosphere of *The Aeneid*. Aeneas does not find it at all easy to fulfill his destiny and perform his duties; he has to be constantly reminded of them and urged on by gods and men to perform them. His true greatness consists in his final fulfillment of those duties in spite of the cost to self. The first six books of *The Aeneid* are in more ways than one a story of wanderings. In them Aeneas is found either actually wandering off or being tempted to wander off from his manifest duties to the gods and to the state. It takes the clear prevision of the greatness of the Rome-to-be, in Book VI, to confirm him in his resolution to march forward unswervingly to his destiny in spite of the grim horrors of cursed war.[5]

This concept of heroic action, of course, is entirely lacking in the excitement and verve of the more irresponsible actions of an Achilles or an Odysseus. The wanderings of Aeneas are entirely devoid of that childlike, fairy-book adventuresomeness that so characterizes the wanderings of Odysseus; and the six books of battles in *The Aeneid* are equally lacking in the youthful bravado that characterizes the battlings of Achilles. There was, after all, no sense of national, much less imperial, urgency about either the wanderings of Odysseus or the warfare of Achilles. The wanderings of Odysseus are predominantly a personal though perilous adventure, and the surge, challenge, and honor of the battlefield are the very breath of life to Achilles. With Aeneas it is quite different. Both his wanderings and his warfare are harsh, heavy duties laid on him by the gods. His greatness consists in his bowing his head to the will of the gods and his shouldering of the heavy duty they have laid upon him to found the new Troy. A seriousness and almost a sadness pervade the whole *Aeneid* that are entirely foreign to both *The Iliad* and *The Odyssey*. The note of sadness is struck early in *The Aeneid* and recurs like a refrain throughout the poem. We first hear it in the very invocation where we get a glimpse of that "fated wanderer," "hard driven on land and on the deep," and "hard bestead in war" (I, p. 1). It was the note which, for some reason or other, Virgil found it easiest to sustain. It rings through the whole fated story of Aeneas from the time that he sadly leaves the burning walls of Troy and the streets flowing with the blood of Priam and his household until the moment when he stands victorious over the bleeding corpse of Turnus outside the flaming walls of Lavinium, which he had vainly tried to spare. And in between there had been a long procession of woes: the loss of his wife, Creüsa; the loss

of ships, and followers, and friends at sea; the death of his
father; the necessity of trampling his love for Dido underfoot;
the farewell to the exiles who lacked the courage to face with
him still greater woes; and finally the horrors of a prolonged
war that he had tried vainly to avoid.[6] "Such a task was it to
found the Roman people." The honor that comes to such heroic
labor is, indeed, of a different brand from that which Achilles
sought.

The picture that we get of Aeneas as he sadly begins his
wanderings in search of the new Troy is symbolic of all those
duties for which the true Roman in all ages was most honored:
"Lord Anchises bids us spread our sails to fortune, and weeping I leave the shores and havens of my country, and the plains
where once was Troy. I sail to sea an exile, and with comrades
and son and the gods of household and state" (III, p. 49). He
is leaving the ruined Troy at the direct command of the gods
and his father Anchises to found a new one. His own comfort
and personal pleasure are henceforth to be sacrificed to the
will of the gods and to the new city and empire that are to
arise. With him as he leaves he carries the city and household
gods; it is to find them a new home that he has been com-
manded by the gods themselves to set out on his wanderings.
With him go his father Anchises, the *pater familias*, and his
son Ascanius, symbols of that continuity of family tradition
that is to be one of the great unifying forces in the Roman
society of the future. Anchises is a venerable link with the
ancient past, and Ascanius is the seed of hope for continuity
into the future. Aeneas is merely a necessary link in that great
chain; his greatest duty is to see that the chain is not broken.
And as the chain is more important than any of its links, so
the future of Rome is more important than the present pleasure
of Aeneas. That is the point Virgil is making throughout *The
Aeneid*. Aeneas really becomes a personification of Roman
duty. That is perhaps the reason why he is less interesting and
less convincingly human than either of those archindividualists,
Achilles and Odysseus. But unless we understand that this is

[55]

what the Romans would have admired, or at least what Virgil would have wanted them to admire, in Aeneas, we are apt to misinterpret both him and the poem in which he is the hero. There is admittedly less danger of misinterpreting Aeneas than there is of misinterpreting Achilles, because Virgil makes it almost impossible to mistake what Aeneas stands for.

He makes it quite clear that Aeneas has a solemn commission from the gods to found a new Troy. Readers of *The Aeneid* learn early in Book I that this is Aeneas' final destiny as they listen to the conversation between Jupiter and Venus. When Aeneas has been cast up on Dido's shore by a tempestuous sea after he has already come within sight of Italy, Venus begins to fear that her son will never fulfill his destiny. Jupiter reassures her in these words:

> "Thy people's destiny abides unshaken. Thine eyes shall see the city of Lavinium, their promised fortress; thou shalt exalt to the starry heaven thy noble Aeneas. . . . He whom thou lovest . . . shall wage a great war in Italy, and crush warrior nations; he shall appoint his people a law and a city."
> —I, p. 9.

But to Aeneas himself the knowledge of his great destiny is revealed only gradually. He gets his first premonition of it in a dream in which the ghost of his brother Hector appears to him at the very moment when the walls of Troy are tumbling in ruin and bids him flee.

> "Fly, goddess-born, and rescue thyself from these flames. . . . Troy commends to thee her holy things and household gods; take them to accompany thy fate; seek for them a city, which, after all the seas have known thy wanderings, thou shalt at last establish in might."—II, p. 32.

But the dream only succeeds in awakening Aeneas to Troy's present dangers. In the face of the disaster that surrounds him he seems perfectly capable of being content with the kind of

glory that would have satisfied Achilles. When he sees that
Troy is doomed, his one thought is to die an honorable death
amid the chaos. He himself describes the scene in his narrative
to Dido.

> "Madly I seize my arms, nor is there much purpose in
> arms; but my spirit is on fire to gather a band for fighting
> and charge for the citadel with my comrades. Fury and wrath
> drive me headlong, and I think how noble is death in arms."
> —II, p. 33.

He rushes madly through the burning city to the house of
Priam, where he finds Helen cowering at an altar and vows
to slay her, in revenge for the havoc she has caused to Troy,
before he himself perishes in the ruins. But his hand is stayed
by his goddess-mother, who gives him his first solemn commission. He is to forgo this mad purpose of revenge upon
Helen, and his madder desire of dying gloriously in defense of
Troy, and bethink himself of the safety of his father, Anchises,
and of his son and wife. "Fear thou no commands of thy
mother, nor refuse to obey her counsels" (II, p. 42). Aeneas
obeys. It is the first step in the direction of the fulfillment of
his destiny. But he has no clear idea yet where that step is
leading him. It will take many more messages from the gods
before he will be sure of his destination and will have the
courage to arrive at it.

But Aeneas obeys this first command. He picks his way
through the ruins of the burning city to his own house, only to
find Anchises adamant in his refusal to abandon Troy. It takes
the omen of Ascanius canopied with flame and the confirming
omens of Jupiter's thunder and shooting star to break down
his stubborn refusal. But convinced at last of the divine will,
Anchises acquiesces in these words:

> "Now, delay is done with: I follow, and where you lead,
> I come, gods of my fathers; save my house, save my grand-

child. Yours is this omen, and in your deity Troy stands. I yield, O my son, and refuse not to pass forth beside thee."
—II, p. 45.

Anchises is yielding to the manifest will of the gods, and pointing to his son and grandson the way down which Roman greatness lies. It is the way of duty—duty to the gods and duty to the state. And from this point on in the story, Aeneas' attitude toward Anchises is a manifestation of that other duty, sacred to all Romans, the duty of a son to the *pater familias*.

Aeneas is given one last manifestation of the will of the gods and a little fuller knowledge of his destiny before he leaves Troy. When he misses Creüsa and plunges back into the flaming city to find her, the ghost of Creüsa herself appears to him and bids him flee to fulfill the will of the gods and his own high destiny.

> "What help is there [she says] in this mad passion of grief, sweet my husband? not without divine influence does this come to pass: nor may it be, nor does the high lord of Olympus allow, that thou shouldest carry Creüsa hence in thy company. Long shall be thine exile, and weary spaces of sea must thou plough; yet thou shalt come to the land Hesperia, where Lydian Tiber flows with soft current through rich and populous fields. There prosperity awaits thee, and a kingdom, and a king's daughter for thy wife."—II, p. 47.

This reveals to Aeneas his destination, part of his destiny there, and the fact that he is not to achieve either until he has suffered through long wanderings at sea.

Once it is clear to Anchises that it is the duty of Aeneas to flee ruined Troy to found a new one, he becomes once more the real *pater familias,* and all the action of the story up to and including the pivotal sixth book is under his guidance and command. With very few exceptions, not enough has been made by critics of the place of Anchises in *The Aeneid*.[7] Virgil no doubt meant Aeneas' relation to him to illustrate that duty of son to the father of the family, which was as sacred to the Roman as his duty to the gods and to the state. From the moment they leave Troy until they have landed in Lavinium it is Anchises who counsels and commands; Aeneas listens and obeys. Anchises' first command is to set sail from Troy. "Lord Anchises bids us spread our sails to fortune," Aeneas relates, "and weeping I leave the shores and havens of my country" (III, p. 49). It is he again who commands the fleet to set sail from the shores of the augurer Helenus' home, where they have been given the omen of the white sow under the ilex wood that would tell them they have reached their destination (III, p. 60). It is Anchises, too, who interprets the augury of the herd of white horses sighted on the shores of Italy. They are an augury of war, he tells Aeneas, but of peace, too, to follow.[8] And then Anchises dies. "Driven over so many tempestuous seas, I lose, alas!" says Aeneas, "the solace of every care and chance, Anchises my sire" (III, p. 69). But, as it turns out, Anchises' death enables him to be of even greater assistance to Aeneas; his ghost impresses upon Aeneas even more profoundly than did the living father his great duty to the gods and to the new Troy. Driven by storm onto the shores of Dido's kingdom, Aeneas is soon headed for the greatest obstacle that is to impede him on his way to his fated destiny to found the new Troy. When he is thoroughly enmeshed in the coils of Dido's love, he is rudely shaken out of his oblivion by the message of Mercury dispatched from Jupiter himself. He is told to cease this loitering in a foreign land and bethink him of "Italy teeming with empire and loud with war," where he is destined "to transmit the line of Teucer's royal blood, and lay all the world beneath his law" (IV, p. 78). The message brings Aeneas to his senses; he assures Dido that he is not his own master, that he has a command from the high gods themselves to sail on "to broad Italy" to found a new city and an empire (IV, p. 81). His love for Dido has to be sacrificed to his duty to the gods and to the city which he is destined to found. Anchises has not been idle while his son has been neglecting his duty. "Often," Aeneas tells the queen, "as the stars lift their fires, the troubled phantom of my father Anchises comes in warning and dread; my boy Ascanius comes and the wrong done to one so dear in cheating him of an Hesperian kingdom and destined fields" (IV, p. 81). His father's phantom has been there to remind him that it is his duty to sacrifice his present pleasure and love for Dido to the will of the gods and to the welfare of his son and the future Hesperian kingdom. There they are again—duty to the gods, to the state, and to the family, that trinity of Roman values.

It is the ghost of Anchises once more that plucks Aeneas out of the despondency which seizes him when, after the funeral games in honor of his father, he watches his ships go up in smoke. Aeneas is so discouraged that, in spite of all the prophecies, omens, and commands of the gods, he is tempted to give up the whole project and settle down for good on this quiet island. It is the ghost of his father who seconds the suggestion made by Nautes to leave those behind who lack the heart for future toils, but to push on himself with those courageous souls who are destined to found the new empire (V, pp. 113–114). And to confirm Aeneas in his sagging resolution, Anchises bids his son seek him out in the underworld, where he will give him a vision of the glory of the Rome to be. Aeneas, in answer to his father's command, plunges into the awesome regions of the nether world. The transitional nature of this visit to the kingdom of Dis is suggested by the greeting of the Sibyl who is to be his guide:

"O thou for whom the great perils of the sea are at last over, though heavier yet by land await thee, the Dardanians shall come to the realm of Lavinium; relieve thy heart of this care; but not so shall they have joy of their coming. Wars, grim wars I discern, and Tiber afoam with streams of blood. A Simois shall not fail thee, a Xanthus, a Dorian camp; another Achilles is already provided in Latium, he too goddess-born."—VI, p. 121.

Not a very reassuring greeting in all conscience. He has finished his Odyssey but he still has a whole grim Iliad before him—Achilles and all. He would need all the encouragement that Anchises could give him to face up to this grim lot. Anchises leads him into the pleasant meadows of Elysium and proceeds to give him a vision of the future glories of his new city that make even the prospect of horrible war tolerable. The whole spectacle of the future grandeur of Rome is unfolded before him with its long procession of mighty emperors. When Anchises had finished showing Aeneas this pageantry of Roman greatness to be, and "kindled his spirit with passion for the glories on their way, he tells him thereafter of the war he next must wage and instructs him of the Laurentine peoples and the city of Latinus, and in what wise he may avoid or endure every burden" (VI, p. 145). With this Anchises' task is finished, and his voice drops out of *The Aeneid*. From this point on Aeneas himself is the *pater familias*. He is now sure of his destiny, and certain of his duty to the gods, to the memory of his father, to his son, and to the glorious Rome-to-be. He never again swerves from that duty even when it means shouldering the hated burdens of war.

Virgil makes it perfectly clear throughout *The Aeneid* that, in his view, the real greatness of Aeneas and of Rome was not prowess on the battlefield but the establishment of an empire in which law, justice, and peace reigned. He has Jupiter state that explicitly in his first reassuring speech to Venus:

> "He shall appoint his people a law and a city. . . . From the fair line of Troy a Caesar shall arise, who shall limit his empire with ocean, his glory with the firmament. . . . The dreadful steel clenched gates of War shall be shut fast; inhuman Fury, his hands bound behind him with an hundred rivets of brass, shall sit within on murderous weapons, shrieking with ghastly blood-stained lips."—I, pp. 9-10.

Pax Romana—that is what Jupiter is prophesying here—one of the great glories of the Rome to be. Anchises is equally explicit,

[61]

in his vision proffered to Aeneas in the underworld, about the true basis of Roman greatness:

> "Be thy charge, O Roman, to rule the nations in thine empire; this shall be thine art, to ordain the law of peace, to be merciful to the conquered and beat the haughty down."
> —VI, p. 144.

These two passages could almost be taken as texts which the last six books of *The Aeneid* develop.

Aeneas comes to Lavinium convinced that he has a divine commission to establish a new kingdom there, and he has the testimony of two fulfilled omens that this is actually the place where he is to settle. Latinus, the king of the place, also knows of his divine commission and is willing to welcome the strangers and give Aeneas his daughter Lavinia in marriage. He has, in fact, been refusing her hand to all other suitors because the advent of the stranger from afar who was to marry her and found a new dynasty in Lavinium had been foretold to him. So agreements are drawn up between Latinus and Aeneas, and it looks as if the new kingdom is going to be established peacefully. And then hell itself breaks loose in the person of the Fury Alecto, "whose delight is in woeful wars, in wrath and treachery and evil feuds" (VII, p. 156). This Fury, "hateful to lord Pluto himself, hateful and horrible to the hell-born sisters," [9] takes complete possession of the Queen Amata and fills her with a venomous hatred of Aeneas. The frenzied Amata and the Fury together stir Turnus to the "accursed fury of war, and wrath over all," and he declares war to the finish on Aeneas and all the Teucrians.

Aeneas, "vexed by the dismal warfare," still tries every possible means of reaching a peaceful settlement with Latinus and Turnus, but Latinus has been won over to the side of Turnus by the frenzied Amata, and his efforts are to no avail. Plunged into the bloody business of the battlefield, Aeneas acquits himself like a hero, but there is none of the exaltation in the blood

[62]

and gore of battle that characterized Achilles. When a delegation from the enemy come asking for a truce to bury their dead, Aeneas makes this characteristic reply.

> "What spite of fortune, O Latins, has entangled you in the toils of war, and made you fly our friendship? Plead you for peace to the lifeless bodies that the battle-lot has slain? I would fain grant it even to the living. Neither have I come but because destiny had given me this place to dwell in; nor wage I war with your people; your king it is who has broken our covenant and preferred to trust himself to Turnus' arms."
> —XI, p. 248.

When a fresh battle has broken out after a truce has been declared and it has been agreed that he is to meet Turnus in single combat, Aeneas restrains the fury of his men with this rebuke. "What is this strife that so spreads and swells? Ah, restrain your wrath! truce is already stricken, and all its laws ordained; mine alone is the right of battle" (XII, p. 281). And when he is finally forced to lay siege to the walls of Latinus' city, he loudly reproaches Latinus, "and takes the gods to witness that he is again forced into battle, that twice now do the Italians choose warfare and break a second treaty" (XII, p. 289).

There is no doubt that Virgil represents Aeneas as hating war. Virgil, the poet of "tilth and woodland," gives his epic hero some of his own detestation of war. War was so distasteful to Virgil that he found it difficult to write of it at all. He several times reinvokes the muse in the last six books, begging for the power to tell of "grim wars, and embattled lines" (VII, p. 147. See also IX, p. 208; and especially XII, p. 286). It was as much a task for Virgil to sing of war as it was for Aeneas to engage in it, and it must be confessed that Aeneas was better as a warrior than Virgil was as a war poet. He really had little heart for the task; and, as Professor Bowra has observed,[10] his catalogues of warriors and their engagements lack all the dash and go of the battle scenes in Homer. But Virgil is expressing a Roman sentiment common to his contemporaries when he condemns war and lauds peace. The Romans were tired of war and longed for a secure peace. Virgil gives to Aeneas the same sentiments about war that Cicero expressed in the *De Officiis* when he said that the only justification for engaging in war is to secure peace.[11]

Virgil not only contrasts Aeneas with battle-loving Achilles but also with wily Odysseus. He is totally unlike Achilles in his love of peace and hatred of war; and his respect for law and treaties sets him apart from the wily Odysseus as well. Virgil's epithets for Achilles and Odysseus well express his attitude toward them. Cruel Achilles, and Ulysses, forger of crime, is what he calls them (II, pp. 25, 29). And in his narrative of the fall of Troy Aeneas gives a revolting picture of both Greek cruelty and deceit.

When the wooden horse is discovered outside the walls, Laocoön warns the Trojans against Greek treachery in these words:

> "Believe you the foe is gone? or think you any Grecian gift is free of treachery? is it thus we know Ulysses? . . . Trust not the horse, O Trojans. Be it what it may, I fear the Grecians even when they offer gifts."—II, p. 25.

And when the guileful story of Sinon is unwound, Aeneas holds it up as a tragic example of Greek treachery in general. "Know now the treachery of the Grecians," he says, "and from a single crime learn them all" (II, p. 26). And he ends the tale of Sinon with these words:

> "So by Sinon's wiles and craft and perjury the thing gained belief; and we were ensnared by treachery and forced tears, we whom neither the son of Tydeus nor Achilles of Larissa, whom not ten years nor a thousand ships brought down."—II, p. 30.

To the Roman, who put so much emphasis on law and the sacred force of the sworn word, this kind of treachery and deceit was especially hateful. No Roman would ever have written an epic revolving around the character of a wily Odysseus.

Equally forthright is Aeneas' condemnation of the cruelty of the Greeks. He pictures Neoptolemus as a match for his father Achilles in cruelty, comparing him to a snake fed on poisonous weeds, as he attacks the helpless household of Priam. The picture of his pursuit of Polites and of his slaughter of the lad before the very eyes of his aged father Priam is perhaps the most vivid picture of unfeeling cruelty in all of literature. Equally shocking is the brutality with which he slays the aged Priam himself. When the old man, distraught by the sight of his son's massacre, hurls his ineffectual spear at Neoptolemus, and tells him he lacks the humanity that even his cruel father showed when he released the body of Hector, Neoptolemus retorts, scornfully:

> "Go with a message to my sire the son of Peleus: remember to tell him of my baleful deeds, and the degeneracy of Neoptolemus. Now die." So saying, he drew him quivering to the very altar, slipping in the pool of his child's blood, and wound his hair in the left hand, while in the right the sword flashed out and plunged to the hilt in his side.—II, p. 40.[12]

What a different ring this incident has on the lips of Aeneas from the sound it had on those of Odysseus, as he delighted Achilles in the underworld with the narrative of his son's massacres. "Many was the man he brought down in mortal combat. I could not tell you all the people he killed in battle for the Argives (*Odyssey*, XI, p. 185). This news, we recall, was the one ray of happiness that broke through the gloom of the underworld to cheer up the saddened Achilles. To Aeneas, on the contrary, such slaughter, rather than deserving congratulation and honor, seems most inhuman and hateful. This is some index of how much the basis of honor had changed in the centuries that intervened between Homer and Virgil.

But perhaps the most dramatic contrast between the Homeric ideal of manhood and the Virgilian one comes at the very end of *The Aeneid*, when Turnus and Aeneas meet in final combat. Here we have the new ideal of social duty challenged by the old ideal of personal honor. For Virgil, and perhaps for any Roman, there was no doubt at all which ideal had to win. There is no question about Virgil's intending Turnus to represent the old ideal—more humanely and less brutally than it was represented by Neoptolemus and Achilles—but the old ideal nonetheless.[13] Turnus' pride has been hurt by Latinus: Lavinia, whom he loves and wishes to marry, has been promised by Latinus to this foreigner, Aeneas; under the command of the gods, it is true, but that does not make the situation any less humiliating to Turnus. He is like Achilles; in fact, he is called a second Achilles by the Sibyl in the underworld.[14] Like Achilles, he is ready to plunge the whole of Italy into war and risk his own life rather than let this slight to him in favor of a foreigner go unchallenged. When Latinus makes his final plea with Turnus to allow a peaceful compromise with Aeneas, to take another maiden from Latium to wife, and to settle down to a peaceful coexistence with the newcomer, this is his final answer to the old king:

> "The care thou hast for me, most gracious lord, for me lay down, I implore thee, and let me purchase honour with death."—XII, p. 273.

It was the same choice that had been put to Achilles—peace with dishonor or death with honor; and Turnus makes the same choice of Achilles—death with honor. The great difference between the treatment of that choice by the two poets is this: for Homer, Achilles had made the right choice; but for Virgil, Turnus' choice was tragically wrong. He has even Turnus himself admit it before the end. When death is staring him in the face at the hands of Aeneas, these are almost his last words: "I have deserved it, nor do I ask for mercy; use thy fortune" (XII, p. 299).

Virgil unquestionably tries to make his reader feel that the values for which Turnus stands are irrevocably opposed to those for which Aeneas stands, and that Turnus has to go. He makes both Dido and Turnus great tragic figures, whose tragedy consists, in the one case, in preferring personal pleasure, and, in the other, personal honor to the will of the gods and to the good of the state.[15] But it would seem that, in the case of both Dido and Turnus, Virgil's sensibilities as a person and as a poet outdid his protestations as a patriot. He elicits so much sympathy for Dido in the farewell episode and for Turnus in the final combat that we are apt to feel more regret at what the triumph of Rome cost than admiration for the triumph itself. We are inclined to have more pity for Dido and Turnus than admiration for Aeneas. I am sure that Virgil, however, with his Ciceronian notions of Roman duty, would not have intended it to be so; but, in *The Aeneid* as we have it, I am afraid it *is* so, at least for modern readers.

The same kind of caution, however, is necessary in interpreting *The Aeneid* as *The Iliad*. The Romans, with their exaggerated emphasis on duty to the state, would not have looked upon the tragedy of either Dido or Turnus with quite as much sympathy as we view it, and they would have felt a great deal more admiration for Aeneas than we can muster. Part of the difficulty that we find in accepting Aeneas as a convincing human being[16] and a completely admirable hero is the fact that the Roman ideal which he represents was neither completely human nor entirely admirable. There was too much subordination of the individual to the state in the Roman ideal. That subordination was often justified by the notion of the "manifest destiny" of great powers or great leaders and by "the will of the gods." But these defenses in practice were too often a mere cloak for ruthless imperialism and tyranny. Before "manifest destiny" and "the will of the gods" no individual had any redress as Turnus had no redress in the face of the claims of Aeneas. In Roman history, as in the history of all empires, the benefit of the state and the will of the gods too often became merely the benefit and will of the emperor. Aeneas as a symbol of Roman empire definitely displays some of that attitude which makes him less admirable to us than he might have been to the Romans themselves.

To make a final comparison between the characters of Achilles and Aeneas, we might say that Achilles in many ways seems to us to be an adolescent and Aeneas a mature man.[17] We can understand and sympathize with both of them because we have all been both of them. The most prominent characteristic of all adolescents is their exaggerated individualism and egocentricity; the first sign of maturity in the life of every man is the moment he begins to realize that he must sacrifice some of his personal wants to the wants and rights of others. The man who never learns that necessity never grows up. It can be granted, nonetheless, that the irresponsible world of the adolescent may be more exciting than that of the social-minded adult. Perhaps that is one reason why the story of Achilles, in spite of its colossal self-centeredness, remains a much more exciting story than that of Aeneas. But the character of Aeneas, with his high sense of duty, is to us unquestionably more admirable than that of Achilles, with his passion for personal honor. C. S. Lewis has, in fact, said that, after Aeneas, the only possible forward movement in the development of the hero is in the direction of the Christian hero.[18] As we shall see in subsequent chapters, that is the direction in which the development did move. The pagan ideals of both Greece and Rome were at times revived in both theory and practice; but the new hero, after Virgil, was the Christian hero.

NOTES

[1] See Chapter Three, page 41.

[2] The translation used throughout is that of J. W. Mackail (London: Macmillan & Company, Ltd., 1937), by permission of the publisher. Again direct citations from this translation in the text

will follow the quotation. General references to *The Aeneid* not quoted specifically will also be indicated in the text.

³ *Iliad*, XX, p. 374. This passage in *The Iliad* is, in fact, the germ of the whole *Aeneid*. In it Poseidon is represented as intervening in Aeneas' foolhardy challenge of Achilles, to save him from death at Achilles' hands because, in the plans of Zeus, he was "destined to survive and to save the House of Dardanus from extinction. . . . The great Aeneas shall be King of Troy and shall be followed by his children's children in the time to come."

⁴ "Aeneas is *pius* but he is not a perfect and ideal man throughout the poem. The indignation which he has excited in more than one critic for his obvious faults shows not that Virgil's idea of goodness was singularly unlike our own but that he chose to show a good man in the making and the means by which he is made. To understand Aeneas we must understand the scheme by which Virgil presents him, a scheme based on the moral views of the Augustan age but modified by Virgil's own beliefs and admirations. The clue to Aeneas is that he is built on a Stoic plan. . . . It [Stoicism] was well suited to an age which hoped to recover from the excesses of an unfettered individualism. The quiet, self-denying, self-sacrificing citizen who was prepared to do what he was told was a type dear to Augustus."—Maurice Bowra, *From Virgil to Milton* (London: Macmillan & Co., Ltd., 1945), pp. 58-59. Reprinted by permission of the author, Macmillan & Co., and St. Martins Press.

⁵ "The Stoics believed that a man is not born good, or as they called it 'wise,' but becomes so through testing, *exercitatio*, by which his natural qualities are brought into practice and his character is strengthened and developed. If he responds rightly to this process, he will in the end find that wisdom which is the same as goodness. What matters is the result, the final state of a man. It does not matter if he makes mistakes provided that he learns from them and becomes wise. The great exemplars of Stoic virtue were Hercules and the Dioscuri, men who spent their lives in performing hard tasks and were in the end exalted to deity by their success in them. Into such a scheme [of Stoic virtue] the career and the character of Aeneas may be fitted. In the first five books of the *Aeneid* he is tested; in the later books he has become wise and good and is a complete man."—Bowra, *op. cit.*, p. 59. It is an adaptation of this Stoic notion of the virtuous life as a warfare that was assimi-

lated into Christian teaching. This can, perhaps, be best seen in the Epistles of Saint Paul. (See especially Epistle to the Ephesians, Chapter 6, verses 11-18.) The fact that this concept of virtue forms some of the skeleton of *The Aeneid* also partly explains why the wanderings and battles of Aeneas so easily became, in the Middle Ages, an allegory of the pilgrimage of every man toward his final destiny in the eternal City of God.

[6] This note of woe is sounded many times by Aeneas himself in the poem, most notably when he stands weeping as he looks upon the story of the fall of Troy emblazoned on the temple doors at Carthage, and when Dido later asks him to tell her the story of those woes and his own wanderings. This is the way he begins his story: "Dreadful, O Queen, is the woe thou bidst me recall, how the Grecians pitiably overthrew the wealth and lordship of Troy; and I myself saw these things in all their horror, and bore a great part in them. . . . Though my spirit shudders at the remembrance and recoils in pain, I will essay" (II, p. 24). This is the way he begins the sad story of the fall of Troy, and equally sad is his preface to the story of his own wanderings. "And here I find a marvellous great company, newly flocked in, mothers and men, a people gathered for exile, a pitiable crowd. From all quarters they are assembled, ready in heart and fortune, to whatsoever land I will conduct them overseas" (II, p. 47).

[7] Theodor Haecker is one of the exceptional critics who does call attention to the place of filial devotion as an important ingredient in Roman *pietas*. "Aeneas is pious, firstly in his capacity as a son. This relationship is the natural home of the Roman *pietas*. To be pious meant to be a 'son,' and lovingly to fulfill the duties of filial relationship. Love fulfilling duties, or rather loving fulfillment of duties, this is the meaning of piety. Himself a Father, the forefather of Caesar and Augustus, Aeneas saw in his own son and his son's son yet other ancestors and fathers of sons who should in their turn be pious toward their fathers and their ancestors. The interchangeable relationship of father and son, and the primacy of the father, is the basis of Virgilian piety. It is not for the sake of his beloved, not to recover the Queen, not to accomplish any heroic feat, but simply for the sake of his father that Aeneas goes down to the underworld, pressing through Hades to the Elysian Fields, where his father welcomes him with tears:

[70]

> *Venisti tandem, tuaque expectata parenti*
> *Vicit itur durum pietas? datur ora tueri*
> *Nate, tua et natas audire et reddere voces.*

To which the son replies:

> *Tua me, genitor, tua tristis imago*
> *Saepius occurrens, haec limina tendere adegit.*

"The source of this piety is the family, and especially the relationship of son to father and father to son, where it is a fond, familiar and simple thing."—From *Virgil, Father of the West,* pp. 62-63, by Theodor Haecker, trs. by A. W. Wheen, published 1934 Sheed and Ward, Inc., New York, New York.

8 "War dost thou carry, land of our sojourn; horses are armed in war, and menace of war is in this herd. But yet these same creatures are wont in time to enter harness, and carry yoke and bit in concord; there is hope of peace too" (III, p. 65).

9 To appreciate Virgil's own attitude toward the madness of war one has only to read this whole passage in Book VII in which Amata and Turnus are themselves gradually turned into semifiends under the poisonous influence of the Fury Alecto.

10 Bowra, as usual, is very clear in his differentiation between Virgil's and Homer's attitude toward war, as the following passage indicates: "Aeneas is very like an invader, and he lives in an heroic past, but he must not be allowed to make war as Homer's heroes make it, simply to indulge his own desire for glory. For this reason Virgil makes Aeneas face war with a consciousness of grave responsibilities and of nice distinctions between moral issues. . . . War has become an evil which may be undertaken only when there is no alternative, and it must be conducted in a spirit of chivalry and clemency."—*Op. cit.,* pp. 64-65.

11 Cicero, *De Officiis,* See Chap. III, p. 47.

12 Bowra says of Virgil as war poet that the only time he becomes enthusiastic is when he is singing of the horrors of war: "At certain places he created a new poetry, which his contemporaries understood and appreciated, about the tragedy and confusion of war. . . . He sees war from the standpoint of a suffering civilian as a chaos of horror and muddle. This standpoint is perfectly human, and there is much tragic beauty as well as eternal truth in Virgil's Sack of Troy. In war horror and muddle inevitably play a

large part, and Virgil added a new realm to poetry when he wrote about them."—*Op. cit.*, p. 41.

¹³ See Bowra, *op. cit.*, pp. 43-49, for an excellent discussion of Turnus as an exemplification of the old Homeric concept of the hero. He closes his discussion with the remark that "he [Turnus] represents that heroic world which contains in its ideals the seeds of its own destruction, and in him Virgil shows that he understood the heroic [Achillean] type and even admired it but knew that it was no longer what the world needed."

¹⁴ These are the words with which the Sibyl describes Turnus to Aeneas in the underworld: "Wars, grim wars I discern, and Tiber afoam with streams of blood. A Simois shall not fail thee, a Xanthus, a Dorian camp; another Achilles is already provided in Latium, he too goddess-born" (VI, p. 121). It is to be the battle of Troy all over again, but this time the Trojans are to be victorious. Turnus, as embodying the old self-centered ideal of the Greeks, is to yield to Aeneas, the embodiment of the new, more social-minded ideal of the Romans.

¹⁵ In this connection it is worth pointing out that Virgil represents both Dido's excessive love and Turnus' passion for honor as madness. Dido has been driven to her madness, it is true, by the wiles of Venus and Cupid, and Turnus to his by the poison of the Fury Alecto; but the point Virgil is making is that the excess in both cases, as an irrational neglect of duty, was mad. Dido's love is referred to as madness in at least a half-dozen places. Thus (IV, p. 73): "How many vows or shrines help her madness"; "As day wanes, she seeks the repeated banquet, and again in her madness pleads to hear the agony of Ilium" (p. 73); "Soon as she [Juno] perceives her thus fast in the toils, and madly careless of her name" (p. 74); "So when, overcome by her pangs, she has caught the madness and resolved to die" (p. 85); "Alas, the fire of madness speeds me on" (p. 82); and finally "For since neither by fate did she perish, nor as one who had earned her death, but woefully before her day, and fired by sudden madness" (p. 92). Dido's tragedy is that she prefers her mad love to her duty to her dead husband and to her newly founded kingdom. Both Aeneas and Dido are described in verse—as "lovers forgetful of their fairer fame" (p. 77). Aeneas is for the time forgetting that his fame lies in founding the new Troy, and Dido is tragically and permanently neglecting her duty

to her dead husband and to the kingdom of which she is queen. She herself is conscious of the neglect at times, as when she says: "O faith ill kept, that was plighted to Sychaeus' ashes" (IV, p. 87); and later: "I have built a renowned city, I have seen ramparts arise; by my brother's punishment, I have avenged my husband of my enemy [this was the basis of her true honor for Virgil and the Romans]; happy, ah me! and over happy, had but the keels of the Dardanians never touched our shores [because then she would never have madly failed in her duty to her kingdom]" (IV, p. 90).

Turnus himself also calls his last conflict with Aeneas madness. This is his last prayer to his sister before he enters into that final combat: "I am resolved to face Aeneas, resolved to bear what bitterness there is in death; nor shalt thou longer see me shamed, sister of mine. Let me be mad, I pray thee, with this madness before the end" (XII, p. 291). Turnus' tragedy is the fact that he prefers his own honor to the declared will of the gods and the good of the new state to be. This is the error he acknowledges in these last words to Aeneas when he is about to be slain: "I have deserved it, nor do I ask for mercy; use thy fortune" (XII, p. 299).

[16] Aeneas, in his devotion to duty, at times seems more of a cold personification of Roman virtue than a warm-blooded human being—an impression which is nowhere more vivid than in his feelingless farewell to Dido in Book VI. But in the one quality of warm sympathy he is very human. His sympathy is evident throughout his story. He is tremendously moved by the sight of the cruel slaughter of Polites and Priam and is reminded by it of the plight of his own defenseless father and son. When Creüsa is lost in the burning city, he is genuinely distraught and risks his life to try to find her. Although he seems singularly unmoved in his farewell to Dido, he was not without sympathy for her as he shows when she refuses to speak to him in the underworld. Finally he *is* touched even by Turnus' final plea, and is almost ready to spare him as he begs for kindness toward his old father, until he sees the girdle of Pallas that Turnus is wearing and is kindled to the wrath that undoes the unfortunate Turnus.

[17] C. S. Lewis, in his *Preface to Paradise Lost* (London: Oxford University Press, 1952, p. 36), is the first to have pointed out this distinction between the characters of Achilles and Aeneas: "*Vicit iter durum pietas;* with this conception Virgil has added a new

dimension to poetry. I have read that his Aeneas, so guided by dreams and omens, is hardly the shadow of a man beside Homer's Achilles. But a man, an adult, is precisely what he is; Achilles had been little more than a passionate boy. You may, of course, prefer the poetry of spontaneous passion to the poetry of passion at war with vocation, and finally reconciled. Every man to his taste. But we must not blame the second for not being the first. With Virgil European poetry grows up."

[18] *Ibid*., p. 38: "In making his one legend symbolical of the destiny of Rome, he has, willy-nilly, symbolized the destiny of Man. His poem is 'great' in a sense in which no poem of the same type as the *Iliad* can ever be great. The real question is whether any epic development beyond Virgil is possible. But one thing is certain. If we are to have another epic it must go on from Virgil. Any return to the *merely* heroic, any lay, however good, that tells merely of brave men fighting to save their lives or to get home or to avenge their kinsmen, will now be an anachronism. You cannot be young twice. The explicitly religious subject for any future epic has been dictated by Virgil; it is the only further development left."

CHAPTER FIVE

The Christian Magnanimous Man

"But he that glorieth, let him glory in the Lord. For not he who commendeth himself, is approved, but he, whom God commendeth."
SAINT PAUL: II Corinthians 10:17, 18

"What hast thou that thou hast not received, And if thou hast received, why dost thou glory as if thou hast not received it?" SAINT PAUL: I Corinthians 4:7

Pope Saint Gregory to Saint Augustine, Apostle to the English: *"And if you remember that you have at any time offended our Creator, either by word or deed, that you always call it to mind, to the end that the remembrance of your guilt may crush the vanity which rises in your heart. And whatsoever you shall receive, or have received, in relation to working miracles, that you consider the same, not as conferred on you, but on those for whose salvation it has been given you."*
THE VENERABLE BEDE: *The Ecclesiastical History of the English Nation*, Book I, Chapter 31

Roman civilization was in many ways a providential preparation for Christianity. The universalism of the Roman Empire had conditioned men to think in world-wide terms which prepared them in some fashion for the advent of a religion, one of whose chief marks was to be its Catholicity. And the great Roman emphasis on duty was a notion that the Christian religion could

[75]

and did appeal to in spreading its new precept of Christian charity.

But one of the greatest difficulties that faced Christ Himself and His Apostles and earliest teachers was making acceptable to the Hebrews and to the Greek and Roman pagans a human ideal that differed rather fundamentally from anything the world had previously known. With the help of occasional prophets sent by God to recall Israel from its wanderings into idolatry, the Hebrew people had, through the centuries, kept alive a belief in the one true God and in a hope for a Messiah or Savior to come. But the Scribes and Pharisees, leaders of the Hebrew people, had more and more come to set their hopes on a Messiah who would restore Israel to a place of political importance in the world. To counteract these false notions and hopes, Christ had to show from His very first appearance that He was a king, indeed, but that His kingdom was not of this world. He had to insist that the kingdom He had come to establish was not a thing of political power and place but a reign in the souls of men who were as meek and humble as Himself. This was a disappointment and a scandal to the proud and ambitious leaders of the Jewish people, and so they contrived the death of this prophet who was so destructive of their hopes for power and pre-eminence in the world.

If, as Saint Paul says (I Cor. 1:22-23), Christ had become a stumbling block even to the Jews, to the Greeks His example of humility and universal charity and forgiveness was mere foolishness. His claims to be divine and yet His refusal to accept the honors and acclaim demanded even by mere earthly kings would have made Christ, in Greek eyes, a kind of apotheosis of the pusillanimous man. A stumbling block to the Jews; to the Greeks, foolishness; and yet the humility and forgiveness of Christ were deliberately chosen by Him because He wished to make crystal clear that the new ideal of human perfection which He had come to establish among men was completely different from both the false ambition of the Hebrews and the false pride of the Greeks. Humility and charity were to be the

[76]

fundamental virtues of the new ideal (Matt. 11:29). On one occasion, He recalled the ancient foundation of this new ideal when He said that the first commandment is that thou shalt love the Lord thy God with thy whole soul, with thy whole heart, and with thy whole mind; and that the second commandment is like unto the first that thou shalt love thy neighbor as thyself (Mark 12:29-31). The first commandment inculcates humility because humility, after all, is nothing more nor less than the recognition of one's dependence upon God, and the second commandment inculcates charity or a respect and love for the dignity of all one's fellow human beings who are made in the image and likeness of God.[1]

For this ideal of universal charity there would have been some vague precedent in the Roman emphasis on duty to the state, to one's family and friends; but Christ's ideal went far beyond that of any Roman or Greek idealist. We have seen that Cicero hinted at a charity that was as broad as the human race itself.[2] But to the dignity of all men as rational creatures, Christ added their incomparably higher dignity as children of God as a motive for loving and honoring them. This new emphasis on the great dignity and worth of every single human individual was a corrective both to the Roman aberration of the total subordination of the individual to the state and to the Greek unlimited self-aggrandizement and pursuit of personal glory.

This, then, was the new Christian ideal in which humility, or dependence upon God, and charity, or duty toward one's neighbor, figured prominently. It was this ideal that Christ sent His Apostles to spread to the ends of the earth. If we read the Apostolic writings and those of the Fathers of the Church, we cannot help being impressed with the universal insistence on these fundamental Christian virtues of humility and charity. Among the Apostolic writers there is no one more insistent on them than Saint Paul. It is particularly significant that he had to place special emphasis on these virtues in his letters to the Corinthians. The very occasion of these letters was a typically Greek manifestation of vanity and pride. The Corinthian Christians had begun to dispute and quarrel with one another about who was the greater among them—those who had been baptized by Apollo, by Cephas, or by the illustrious Saint Paul. Saint Paul chides them for their idle vanity and takes the occasion of instructing them in the true idea of Christian humility and charity. The only basis for true honor for them is their incorporation with Christ through baptism, and it makes no difference who administers it. If they gloried in their baptism in Christ rather than in the supposed dignity of the minister from whom they received it, he tells them, they would be drawn together in Christian charity rather than torn asunder by envy and idle bickering. In this context he makes what are perhaps some of the most striking statements about the true Christian basis of glory and honor in all of Scripture. (See especially I Corinthians, Chapters 1-4 and 13, and II Corinthians, Chapters 10-13.) It is true, he says, that he, Paul, has planted the seed of faith in their hearts and that Apollo has fostered it, but God alone has made it fruitful. Therefore to God alone is due the honor and neither to himself nor to Apollo (I Cor. 3:6-7).

This is fundamental to the Christian attitude toward honor. The fact that *all* that a man has both in the natural and supernatural orders he has from God should prevent him from overweening pride in their possession. "What hast thou that thou hast not received," Saint Paul asks in another place, "and if thou hast received, why dost thou glory, as if thou hadst not received?" (I Cor. 4:7.)

In Chapter 12 of the Second Epistle to the Corinthians, Saint Paul refers to the visions that had been given him by God, in which he was snatched up into the seventh heaven; but he asserts that certainly these visions are no basis of personal glory to himself. As gifts of God, they redound to the honor and glory of God, who gave them to him. So it is with other accomplishments of which anyone might be tempted to boast. They are all gifts of God; and, if men are honored for them, at least God should be equally honored as their source. And Saint Paul also insists that whatever special gifts God has granted him were not granted for his own personal benefit alone but that they might be employed in the service of his neighbor.

It is worth recalling here the great emphasis, in the First Letter to the Corinthians, that Saint Paul places on charity as a mark of the true Christian spirit. The famous Chapter 13 of First Corinthians is a paean of praise to the great virtue of charity. But in that song of praise Saint Paul also condemns practically all the self-centered traits of the Greek magnanimous man.

> If I speak with the tongues of men and of angels, and have not charity, I am become as sounding brass, or a tinkling cymbal.
>
> And if I should have prophecy and should know all mysteries, and all knowledge, and if I should have all faith, so that I could remove mountains, and have not charity, I am nothing.
>
> And if I should distribute all my goods to feed the poor, and if I should deliver my body to be burned, and have not charity, it profiteth me nothing.
>
> Charity is patient, is kind: charity envieth not, dealeth not perversely; is not puffed up;
>
> Is not ambitious, seeketh not her own, is not provoked to anger, thinketh no evil;
>
> Rejoiceth not in iniquity, but rejoiceth with the truth.
> —I Cor. 13:1-6.

A recognition that all the good one has comes from God and that to Him, therefore, should go the greater glory, and a willingness to use all that one has for the benefit of one's neighbor—these constitute in Saint Paul the ground plan for the great structure of Christian heroism that was to be built in every succeeding century of the Christian Era.

But as unmistakable as these virtues are in the teachings of Christ and the Apostles, it was a perennial problem for the successors of Christ and the Apostles to make them understood and accepted as marks of the true Christian. And this difficulty obtained whether the Apostles were directing themselves to members of the Greco-Roman world or to barbarians outside the pale of that civilization. To be effective they had to appeal to and preserve as much in the pagan world they were addressing as they possibly could. As we have seen, there were elements in the Roman view particularly that could work as a foundation for the new virtues: the Roman sense of subordination of the individual to the gods and to the State could, with a radical shift of object and motivation, be transformed into the Christian concept of humility; and the even stronger Roman sense of duty could be expanded and elevated into the concept of Christian charity. And there were similar values among the barbarians of the North to which the Christian missioners could and did appeal to make the new ideal intelligible and acceptable. Even the Roman historian Tacitus is at pains to point out to his Roman readers in his *Germania*[3] some of the distinctive mores of the Germanic people that set them apart from most Romans. Of the virtues listed, these Tacitus sets down as most characteristic of the northern peoples: the almost exaggerated sense of service and loyalty of the *comitatus* to the chief of the tribe, a remarkable reverence and respect for women, and an extraordinary sense of hospitality and friendship manifested in mutual gift giving. It was particularly on the ideal of service and loyalty of the *comitatus* to the chief that the Christian concept of humility or subordination of the individual to God could be grafted, and the instinct for unquestioning hospitality and service to the neighbor could be easily extended and elevated to embrace the notion of Christian charity.

Prudent Christian missioners in the northern countries were not slow to capitalize on the features of the native ideals and practices that could facilitate the acceptance of new Christian ideals and practices—and this with the sanction of highest authority. It is interesting in this connection to cite the advice of Pope Saint Gregory to Saint Augustine concerning the most prudent and profitable methods of evangelizing the Britons. Evidently Saint Augustine, as a new broom, had been sweeping a little bit too cleanly, and Gregory reminds him in a letter to the Abbot Melitus, whom he is sending him as a helper, that it is neither necessary nor prudent to sweep out all native custom and ideology.

"When, therefore, Almighty God shall bring you to the most reverend Bishop Augustine, our brother, tell him what I have, upon mature deliberation on the affair of the English, determined upon, viz., that the temples of the idols in that nation ought not to be destroyed; but let the idols that are in them be destroyed; let holy water be made and sprinkled in the said temples, let altars be erected, and relics placed. For if those temples are well built, it is requisite that they be converted from the worship of devils to the service of the true God; that the nation, seeing that their temples are not destroyed, may remove error from their hearts, and knowing and adoring the true God, may the more familiarly resort to the places to which they have been accustomed. And because they have been used to slaughter many oxen in the sacrifices to devils, some solemnity must be exchanged for them on this account, as that on the day of the dedication, or the nativities of the holy martyrs, whose relics are there deposited, they may build themselves huts of the boughs of trees, about those churches which have been turned to that use from temples, and celebrate the solemnity with religious feasting, and no more offer beasts to the Devil, but kill cattle to the praise of God in their eating, and return thanks to the Giver of all things for their sustenance; to the end that, whilst some gratifications are outwardly permitted them, they may the more easily consent to the inward consolations of the grace of God. For there is no doubt that it is impossible to efface every thing at once from their obdurate minds; because he who endeavours to ascend to the highest place, rises by degrees or steps, and not by leaps. Thus the Lord made Himself known to the people of Israel in Egypt; and yet He allowed them the use of the sacrifices which they were wont to offer to the Devil, in his own worship; so as to command them in his sacrifice to kill beasts, to the end that, changing their hearts, they might lay aside one part of the sacrifice whilst they retained another; that whilst they offered the same beasts which they were wont to offer, they should offer them to God, and not to idols; and thus they would no longer be the same sacrifices. Thus it behoves your affection to communicate to our aforesaid brother, that he, being there present, may consider how he is to order all things." [4]

So much did Saint Augustine and his successors take this advice of Pope Saint Gregory to heart that the story of practically all of Anglo-Saxon literature and art is an interesting mixture of the ancient native and the new Christian ideology and motif. This is true whether one is studying Anglo-Saxon sculpture, book illumination, or poetry. [5]

In another letter sent directly to Saint Augustine, Gregory sketches for him, in almost Pauline terms, the example of Christian humility and charity that he ought to set for his flock. Word has come to Gregory of Saint Augustine's procession of miracles, and this is the paternal advice that the news occasions.

"I know, most loving brother, that Almighty God, by means of your affection, shows great miracles in the nation which He has chosen. Wherefore it is necessary that you rejoice with fear, and tremble whilst you rejoice, on account of the same heavenly gift; viz., that you may rejoice because the souls of the English are by outward miracles drawn to inward grace; but that you fear, lest, amidst the wonders that are wrought, the weak mind may be puffed up in its own presumption, and as it is externally raised to honour, it may thence inwardly fall by vainglory. For we must call to mind, that when the disciples returned with joy after preaching, and said to their heavenly Master, 'Lord, in thy name, even the devils are subject to us'; they were presently told, 'Do not rejoice on this account, but rather rejoice for that your names are written in heaven.' For they placed their thoughts on private and temporal joys, when they rejoiced in miracles; but they are recalled from the private to the public, and from the temporal to the eternal joy, when it is said to them, 'Rejoice for this, because your names are written in heaven.' For all the elect do not work miracles, and yet the names of all are written in heaven. For those who are disciples of the truth ought not to rejoice, save for that good thing which all men enjoy as well as they, and of which their enjoyment shall be without end.

"It remains, therefore, most dear brother, that amidst those things, which through the working of our Lord, you outwardly perform, you always inwardly strictly judge yourself, and clearly understand both what you are yourself, and how much grace is in that same nation, for the conversion of which you have also received the gift of working miracles. And if you remember that you have at any time offended our Creator, either by word or deed, that you always call it to mind, to the end that the remembrance of your guilt may crush the vanity which rises in your heart. And whatsoever you shall receive, or have received, in relation to working miracles, that you consider the same, not as conferred on you, but on those for whose salvation it has been given you." [6]

This passage invites comparison with Chapters 10-13 of Saint Paul's Second Epistle to the Corinthians. It is surcharged with the same humble realization of one's entire dependence upon God for all that one is and has and of the fact that whatever one has he has from God not entirely for himself but also in trust for one's neighbor.

This is the charter of the Christian ideal of conduct as Saint Gregory entrusted it to the Apostle of Britain. It was an ideal that was assimilated in varying degrees into the life and literature of these new Christians on the northern fringe of Christendom. As the next chapter will attempt to demonstrate, the *Beowulf* poet, writing for an audience that was quite familiar with both the Germanic and the Christian traditions, takes the outline of his story from the ancient native tradition, but subtly changes the characters, action, and motivation of the story to illuminate the new Christian ideal. But in doing so he does not destroy the old. *Beowulf* is so unquestionably a product of a culture separate from that of the classical and Mediterranean South that is has sometimes been taken to be completely pagan. The *Beowulf* poet, like Saint Augustine acting on the advice of Saint Gregory, does not sweep his temple clean of all the Nordic past but only of that which is entirely incompatible with the new ideal he is enshrining there. Like Saint Augustine and his successors, he found much that did not have to go.

NOTES

[1] Saint John is called in the Gospels themselves the disciple whom Jesus loved (John 21:7). And none of the Evangelists is more insistent than he on Christ's message of fraternal charity as the mark of the true Christian. It is he who recounts Christ's wonderful discourse on love at the Last Supper (Chapters 13-16), and in his epistles he emphasizes this new commandment almost to the point of monotony. The following is only one from among many statements on the subject which he makes in the epistles: "If any man say, I love God, and hateth his brother; he is a liar. For he that loveth not his brother whom he seeth, how can he love God, whom he seeth not? And this commandment we have from God, that he, who loveth God, love also his brother" (I John 4:20-21). The particular newness in Christ's commandment of brotherly love was the universal extent of that love. Fraternal charity had been a great point in the Old Law, too, but it was an exclusive charity extending only to the Hebrews themselves and notoriously excluding such people as the despised Samaritans. Christ, by word and example, had to break through this exclusiveness and inculcate a charity that included even one's enemies. "You have heard that it hath been said, Thou shalt love thy neighbor, and hate thy enemy. But I say to you, Love your enemies: do good to them that hate you: and pray for them that persecute and calumniate you: that you may be the children of your Father Who is in heaven, Who maketh his sun to rise upon the good, and bad, and raineth upon the just and the unjust. For if you love them that love you, what reward shall you have? do not even the publicans this? And if you salute your brethren only, what do you more? do not also the heathens this? Be you therefore perfect as also your

heavenly Father is perfect" (Matt. 5:43-48). One could hardly get a clearer and more explicit abrogation of the old pagan self-assertive and self-centered human ideals than this.

2 See above, page 45.

3 Tacitus, *On Britain and Germany*, translated by H. Mattingly; Penguin Classics (Harmondsworth, Eng.: Penguin Books, Ltd., 1954), Chaps. 7-27.

4 The Venerable Bede, *The Ecclesiastical History of the English Nation*, Everyman Edition (London: E. P. Dutton & Co., 1922), pp. 52-53.

5 I have shown in an article entitled *"Beowulf*, An Allegory of Salvation?" soon to be published in *The Journal of English and Germanic Philology*, how this combination of Germanic and Christian motif was employed for allegorical purposes in Anglo-Saxon book illuminations and in Anglo-Saxon and Anglo-Norman religious sculpture.

6 Bede, *op. cit.*, pp. 54-55.

CHAPTER SIX

Beowulf, Christian Hero

HROTHGAR TO BEOWULF: *"Now, through the might of the Lord, a warrior has done a deed which up to now we all could not accomplish by our schemings. Lo! That self-same woman who bore this child among the tribes of men may say, if she still lives, that the eternal God has been gracious to her in her childbearing."* Beowulf, l. 939

BEOWULF TO HROTHGAR: *"Behold, we have brought thee with gladness, O son of Healfdene, ruler of the Scyldings, these sea-spoils which thou lookest on here, in token of success. I narrowly escaped with my life in fight under the water; I dared the work with difficulty; almost had my struggling ceased, if God had not protected me. I could do nothing in the fray with Hrunting, trusty though that weapon be. Howbeit the Ruler of men granted me that I might see hanging in beauty on the wall a huge old sword."* Beowulf, l. 1651

"He had been of earthly kings the mildest and gentlest of men, the kindest to his people and the most eager for fame." Beowulf, l. 3180

The epic *Beowulf*, like *The Iliad* and *The Odyssey*, fell victim to the nineteenth-century critics who insisted that each of the three poems was a product not of one but of several hands. In the case of *Beowulf*, along with this multiple-authorship theory, there generally went the notion that it was a substantially pagan poem into which later Christian interpolations had been introduced.[1] Today both notions are rather universally discounted. Such outstanding *Beowulf* scholars as R. W. Chambers, Frederick Klaeber, and Charles W. Kennedy are all agreed that the poem is in spirit thoroughly Christian. Klaeber was the first to insist on the point in several articles and in the scholarly introduction to his edition of the poem.

Predominantly Christian are the general tone of the poem and its ethical viewpoint. We are no longer in a genuine pagan atmosphere. The sentiment has been softened and purified. The virtues of moderation, unselfishness, consideration for others are practised and appreciated. The manifest readiness to express gratitude to God on all imaginable occasions, and the poet's sympathy with weak and unfortunate beings like Scyld the foundling and even Grendel and his mother, are typical of the new note. Particularly striking is the moral refinement of the two principal characters, Beowulf and Hrothgar. Those readers who, impressed by Beowulf's martial appearance at the beginning of the action, expect to find an aggressive warrior hero of the Achilles or Sigfrit type, will be disposed at times to think him somewhat tame, sentimental, and fond of talking. Indeed the final estimate of the hero's character by his own faithful thanes lamenting his death is chiefly praise of Beowulf's gentleness and kindness: *cwædon þæt hē wære wyruldcyning[a]/manna mildust ond monðwærust,/lēodum liðost ond lofgeornost 3180.*

The Christian elements are almost without exception so deeply ingrained in the very fabric of the poem that they cannot be explained away as the work of a reviser or later interpolator. In addition, it is instructive to note that whilst the episodes are all but free from those modern [Christian] influences, the main story has been thoroughly imbued with the spirit of Christianity. It is true, the action itself is not modified or visibly influenced by Christianization. But the quality of the plot is changed. The author has fairly exalted the fights with fabled monsters into a conflict between the powers of good and evil.[2]

[87]

Chambers was equally explicit about it in his *Beowulf, An Introduction* and later in his admirable essay entitled "Beowulf and the Heroic Age."

> The vagueness which is so characteristic of the Christian references in *Beowulf* [they may not have been nearly as vague to the Beowulf poet's audience as they seem to the modern critics] can then hardly be due to the poem having originally been a heathen one, worked over by a Christian.
>
> Others have seen in this vagueness a proof "that the minstrels who introduced the Christian element had but a vague knowledge of the new faith [Chadwick]": or that the poem was the work of "a man who, without having, or wanting to have, much definite instruction, had become Christian because the Court had newly become Christian [Clark Hall]." But vague as it is, does the Christianity of *Beowulf* justify such a judgment as this? Do not the characters of Hrothgar or of Beowulf, or of Hygd or of Wealhtheow, show a Christian influence which, however little dogmatic, is anything but superficial? [3]

And later in the same work Chamber says:

> The great merit of *Beowulf* as a historic document is that it shows us a picture of a period in which the virtues of the heathen "Heroic Age" were tempered by the gentleness of the new belief; an age warlike, yet Christian: devout, yet tolerant.[4]

And in what is undoubtedly one of the most discerning essays ever written on the poem, Chambers has this to say:

> Now in Anglo-Saxon England this Heroic Age was brought into contact with Christianity, and with all the civilization of the Mediterranean which came to England with Christianity.
>
> It is just this which makes the Seventh Century in England so exciting an epoch. Christian gentleness, working upon the

passions of the Heroic Age, produces at once a type which is the rough outline of what later becomes the medieval ideal of the knight, or the modern ideal of the gentleman.[5]

Most recently the point has been made again by Professor Kennedy in the introduction to his translation of the poem.

> We have seen that the primitive material of the *Beowulf* was derived from pagan folk-tale, chronicle, and legend, and slowly welded into new unities. It remained for the Old English poet to complete this process of fusion by the conversion, or transmutation, of this material from pagan to Christian. The epic emerges at last as a Christian poem. This mutation, moreover, is not merely a matter of altered phrases, or of interpolated references to the Christian faith, but is a deeply pervasive infusion of Christian spirit coloring thought and judgment, governing motive and action, a continuous and active agent in the process of transformation.[6]

That *Beowulf* is a Christian rather than a pagan poem is, therefore, by no means a new idea. Nor is the idea that Beowulf himself is a Christian rather than a pagan hero new. Kennedy has been emphatic on the point.

> Though Beowulf has a remote prototype in the laggard younger son of folk-tale and has been accorded a place in the succession of Geatish kings, his character has been recast and developed in the spirit of the Christian tradition. Throughout the poem divine guidance is invoked, and acknowledged, as the assisting force by which the heroic deeds of Beowulf are accomplished. After his death his fame is celebrated not only, and not most, for valor and venturous deeds, but for the gentler qualities of Christian virtue.[7]

There is nothing new, then, in seeing Beowulf as a Christian hero; but it seems to me that the extent of his Christian spirit is seen with new clarity when his character and actions are examined in the light shed upon them by the Christian notion

[89]

of magnanimity. Such a scrutiny reveals how completely Beowulf exemplifies the virtue of magnanimity as Christian writers in all ages conceived it. These writers are willing to admit, with Saint Paul, that in itself there is nothing wrong in the great man's seeking honor as long as that pursuit is limited by two things: the clear recognition and admission (1) that whatever he has that merits honor he has from God, that whatever he achieves he achieves with the providential help of God, and that, therefore, to God should go the greater honor and glory; and (2) that all the talents and powers that have made him great were given him not for himself alone but in order that he might employ them in the service of his neighbor as well as of himself. In other words, the true Christian can never make the pursuit of honor an unqualified end in life; it must always be limited by humility, or the recognition of his dependence upon God for all that he is and all that he does, and by charity, or the recognition that he is his brother's keeper and that he cannot, therefore, ignore his brother's rights and needs in the pursuit of his own personal honor and glory. The Christian notion of honor so circumscribed by the Christian virtues of humility and charity loses the excessive selfishness and egotism of the Greek ideal and becomes one of the clearest norms for distinguishing the Christian from pagan values in both literature and life. When that norm is employed to interpret Beowulf, the extent to which his character and actions were created under the new influence of the "gentler qualities of Christian virtue" becomes very much more apparent.

The first prerequisite for the magnanimous man, we recall, in any conception of him, is that he be a man of genuine heroic stature, pre-eminent in all the virtues. Even a cursory reading of *Beowulf* makes it clear that the *Beowulf* poet has striven to give his hero pre-eminence in both physical and spiritual qualities. Over and over again he is described as "the strongest of men," towering over all his followers in physical stature, and with a handgrip of thirty men. All his own brag speeches and the various flashbacks upon his past exploits reveal him as a man of almost giant strength and matchless courage. But besides his physical prowess, Beowulf is consistently represented as possessed of an innate nobility of character that wins him the instinctive respect of followers, friends, and strangers alike. When he comes to the land of the Danes, the herald declares that he has never seen a nobler man than Beowulf. "Never have I seen a mightier noble upon earth, a warrior in armour, than is one of you; that is no retainer dignified by weapons, unless his countenance, his peerless form belies him." [8] And later, when he announces the newcomers to King Hrothgar, the herald says of Beowulf: "Assuredly the chief is doughty who has led these battle-heroes hither." [9] As he appears at the beginning of the poem—mighty, brave, and virtuous—so he is described at the end when he goes forth fearlessly to meet the firedrake:

> Then rose the doughty champion by his shield; bold under his helmet, he went clad in his war-corslet to beneath the rocky cliffs, and trusted to his own strength—not such is the coward's way. Then he, who, excellent in virtues, had lived through many wars,—the tumult of the battles, when armies clashed together,—saw by the rampart a rocky arch whence burst a stream out from the mound; hot was the welling of the flood with deadly fire.[10]

And in this last deadly conflict, Beowulf acquits himself as the mighty, brave, and noble hero he has been pictured to be throughout the poem.

A superficial reading of the poem might suggest that Beowulf in all his exploits was dominated by the very same motives that prompted Achilles. The very last words of the poem sung in praise of their hero by his loyal followers describe him as a man "most eager for fame." [11] And several times in the course of the poem fame as a motive of Beowulf's actions comes to the fore, either in the speeches of the hero himself or in the remarks of those who surround him. The greeting of Hrothgar's herald, Wulfstan, is somewhat ambiguous, but, taken by itself, it might seem to have the old heroic ring: "I believe you have sought out Hrothgar, not from exile, but from prowess and from loftiness of spirit." [12] Again in Beowulf's first brag speech to Hrothgar, we seem to be hearing nothing different from the boastful self-confidence of Achilles:

> "I have in my youth undertaken many deeds of daring. . . . My people, the noble and wise men, advised me thus, Lord Hrothgar,—that I should visit thee, because they knew the strength of my might. They had themselves looked on, when, blood-stained from battles, I returned from the fight, where I bound five, laid low a brood of giants, and slew by night sea-monsters on the waves. . . . And now I will decide the matter alone against the monster, the giant, Grendel! . . . Moreover, I have learnt that in his rashness the monster recks not of weapons. Hence,—so that Hygelac, my prince, may be glad at heart on my account, I renounce that I should bear a sword, or ample shield, or yellow buckler to the battle; but with the fiend I will close with grip of hand, and contend for our lives, foe against foe." [13]

On the face of it, this seems to be as arrogant a boast as any that Achilles ever made. And in a like tone Beowulf later tells the gracious Queen Wealtheow that he will display his courage against the monster Grendel or die in the attempt: "I will show the courage of a hero, or in this mead-hall pass my latest day."[14] Love of fame seems also to be the motive which even Hrothgar appeals to when he wishes the hero success in his adventure.

> "Take now and guard this best of houses, be mindful of thy fame, make known thy mighty valour, watch against the foe. Thou shalt lack nothing what thou wilt, if thou doest escape this bold adventure with thy life." [15]

And when Beowulf has been successful in the adventure and the defeated Grendel slinks away to his lair to die, the fact is recorded in these terms: "Glory in fight was granted to Beowulf." [16] Later, when Grendel's mother has revenged herself for the death of her son by making off with one of the Danes, Beowulf assures Hrothgar that he will seek her out and either win glory by slaying her or die a noble death in the attempt. "Each of us must expect an end of living in this world," he says, "let him who may win glory before death: for that is best at last for the departed warrior." [17] And again when Beowulf is in mortal combat with the fierce dam of Grendel, glory in the fight seems to be his one thought. When he finds that his sword is useless, he faces the troll fearlessly, relying on the strength of his handgrip. "So must a man do when he thinks to win enduring fame in war," observes the poet, "he will have no care about his life." [18] And not only was fame in battle an important consideration for the young Beowulf; as an old man he still seems eager to win renown by combat with the firedrake. These are the opening words of his last brag speech:

> "I ventured on many battles in my younger days; once more will I, the aged guardian of the people, seek combat and get renown, if the evil ravager will meet me outside his earthy vault." [19]

And the poet describes Beowulf in the very midst of the deadly fray with the fire-spouting dragon as "mindful of glorious deeds." [20] It would seem, then, from all this that in Beowulf we have another example of the self-centered pursuit of glory that puts him in the company of Achilles. The character of Beowulf has sometimes been so interpreted.[21]

But so to interpret him is to ignore the consistent qualifications that the *Beowulf* poet puts on his hero's pursuit of glory all through the poem. Those qualifications, we shall see, are the identical ones enumerated by Saint Paul in his Second Epistle to the Corinthians and by Pope Saint Gregory in his letter to Saint Augustine—the recognition of one's dependence upon God for all one's talents and the employment of those talents not merely or primarily for oneself but for one's neighbor.

Reference to one providential God Who created and governs all, and Who will eventually judge all men is persistent throughout the poem. It is to this one providential God and Lord of all that Beowulf gives all the credit for his achievements, great and small. When he and his men land in Denmark, their first act, after they have drawn their ships up on the shore, is an act of thanksgiving to God for their safe arrival.[22] When Beowulf makes his first speech at the court of Hrothgar and assures the old king that he is ready to challenge the monster Grendel, he resigns himself to the will of God in the outcome: "He whom death carries off shall resign himself to God's judgment." [23] As he prepares himself for the advent of the monster, he is described by the poet as trusting firmly "in his proud might, the favor of the Creator." [24] Here the poet seems definitely to be introducing the Christian notion that whatever one has he has as a gift from the Creator. Beowulf himself explicitly recognizes the providential disposition of God in his regard when he declares that he will not use arms against Grendel, who is ignorant of the clash of weapons.

> "But we two at night shall not make use of swords, if he dare seek combat without arms; and then may the wise God, the holy Lord, decree the triumph to whichever side seems meet to Him." [25]

The poet's comment, as Beowulf and his men prepare their beds in the ill-fated hall of Heorot, again recognizes the all-pervading influence of Divine Providence upon the actions and destinies of Beowulf and his men.

> But to the people of the Geats, the Lord gave the weavèd destiny of success in war,—help and support, so that they should all overcome their enemy through the power of one man, through his own strength. It is known for certain that God Almighty has always ruled over the race of men.[26]

Later, when Beowulf himself describes his struggle with Grendel, he also acknowledges God's providential part in the outcome. He could not prevent Grendel from escaping to his lair because God did not will it. "I could not keep him from going, the Creator did not will it," [27] are the hero's own words. But for all that, Beowulf is sure that Grendel will not escape the final judgment of God: "Thus shall the creature stained with crime wait for the Last Judgment;—how the glorious Creator will sentence him!" [28] When, in turn, the poet is summing up Beowulf's first great exploit against Grendel, he is most explicit in having Beowulf acknowledge that all his power is from God:

> He bore in mind the power of his might, the lavish gift which God had granted him, and trusted himself to the Lord for grace, help, and support. Hence he had overcome the foe, struck down the demon of hell.[29]

As in the conflict with Grendel so also in that with Grendel's dam, Beowulf's victory is attributed to the providential help of God. Then in the struggle with the water troll "the son of Ecgtheow, the hero of the Geats, would have perished under the wide earth, had not his war-corslet, his strong coat of mail, furnished him succour, and the holy God, the all-wise Lord, brought about victory in battle. With ease, the Ruler of the heavens decided it aright." [30] And Beowulf again is himself represented as quite aware of his dependence upon the providence of God for this second victory. "I dared the work with difficulty," he tells Hrothgar, "almost had my struggling ceased, if God had not protected me." [31] And when he has returned home in triumph, the poet describes the hero as guarding "with the greatest human art the liberal gifts which God had granted him." [32] The aged Beowulf is of the same mind as the young. When he has slain the dragon at the cost of his own life and won the treasure-hoard for his people, he acknowledges again that he would have been helpless against his fiery adversary if God had not helped him. These are almost his last words in the poem: "I utter in words my thanks to the Ruler of all, the King of Glory, the everlasting Lord, for the treasures which I gaze upon, in that I have been allowed to win such things for my people before my day of death!" [33] Wiglaf, Beowulf's one faithful follower in his last combat, is equally explicit in acknowledging the providence of God in his master's behalf. "God, master of victories, granted him that single handed he might avenge himself with the sword." [34] And the poet's own final comment is in a similar vein. The grief and faithful administrations of Wiglaf could not save Beowulf from death: "He could not keep on earth the chieftain's spirit, much though he wished it, nor alter anything ordained by the Almighty. For men of all degrees God's judgment ruled their deeds, just as it still does." [35] Whether we consider the words of the hero himself, or the remarks of other characters in the story, or the comments of the poet, the impression is always the same: all that the hero achieves he achieves with the help and through the grace of a providential God.

But striking as is Beowulf's recognition of his dependence upon God for all that he is and does, the degree in which this Christian idea pervades the poem becomes even more apparent when we consider Hrothgar's attitude toward this matter in the first two episodes. Hrothgar is an old man who has learned much from the experience of years, and there are two things that he has learned in particular: that whatever happens to man happens under the guidance of a providential God, and that a man can achieve nothing without the help of God. When he hears of Beowulf's arrival, he is confident that "the holy God has of his mercy sent him to us West-Danes . . . to meet the terror of Grendel." [36] When he recounts to Beowulf the ravages that Grendel has made upon his followers, he also declares his confidence in God's providential help: "God can easily restrain the wild ravager from his deeds." [37] The old king, in fact, looks upon Beowulf as the instrument of God's providence in saving the Danes from the ravager. And when Grendel has finally been done to death by the mighty grip of Beowulf, Hrothgar speaks with a true Christian instinct when he gives glory to God rather than to Beowulf himself—to the God who had given such might to man. His prayer of thanksgiving is worth citing at length because it expresses so admirably the Christian attitude toward great achievement:

> "For this sight [Grendel's arm] let thanksgiving rise at once to the Almighty! Many horrors and afflictions have I endured through Grendel: Yet God, the King of Glory, can ever work wonder on wonder. It was but now that I despaired of ever seeing a remedy for any of my troubles, since the best of houses stood stained with the blood of battle,—an all-embracing woe for every one of the counsellors, of those who despaired of ever guarding the fortress of this people from foes, from demons and evil spirits. Now, through the might of the Lord, a warrior has done a deed which up to now we all could not accomplish by our schemings. Lo! That self-same woman who bore this child among the tribes of men may say, if she still lives, that the eternal God has been gracious to her in her childbearing." [38]

Hrothgar is perfectly aware of the personal achievement of Beowulf and goes on to acknowledge it, but he first acknowledges the fact that whatever Beowulf had achieved he had achieved through the power and help of God. That granted, there is no limit to the honor he is willing to show Beowulf himself:

> "Now, Beowulf, best of men, in my heart will I love thee as a son; henceforth keep well this new kinship. Thou shall lack no earthly objects of desire of which I have control. Full oft I have assigned a recompense for less,—honour by gifts,—and to a lesser hero, a weaker in the fray. Thou hast brought to pass for thyself by thy exploits, that thy fame shall live for ever and ever. May the Almighty requite thee with good, as he did but now!" [39]

It is natural for this experienced old man to fear that the young and successful Beowulf might be tempted to forget the fact that what he had achieved he had achieved through the providential help of God. We have already seen that Beowulf had not forgotten it, but the circumstances make Hrothgar's worries natural and understandable. In this light his final exhortation to Beowulf on humility, so far from being the foreign interpolation that some scholars have made it, is completely natural and germane to the characters and instincts of both Hrothgar and Beowulf as they have been displayed throughout the poem. He begins by congratulating Beowulf on the fact that his great victories have not puffed him up with false pride: "Beowulf, my friend, thy fame is raised on high over each nation far and wide. Thou doest carry all this might of thine with calmness and discreetness of spirit." [40] The ordinary road to pride is through power and wealth, which lead a man to rely solely on himself and forget that he is dependent upon God, who has given him all that he has. Beowulf is enjoying the heady wine of victory that his great strength has won him and is about to be enriched by the many treasures which Hrothgar has promised him. The aged Hrothgar, experienced in the ways of the human heart, is rejoiced that Beowulf's success has not gone to his head; but loving him as a son, he is anxious that he continue in his same humility of spirit. So what would be more natural, in these circumstances, than an exhortation on humility. As several scholars have pointed out,[41] it takes the form of many a medieval sermon.

It begins with an exemplum—the story of the successful Danish warrior Heremod, who let his success develop into an arrogant and murderous spirit that destroyed many of his Danish companions and which was eventually his own undoing.

"Although the Almighty God exalted him above all men with the joys of power and strength, and helped him on, still there grew up within his heart a savage spirit; never gave he presents to the Danes, that he might obtain glory. Joyless he lived, so that he suffered misery for his violence, the lasting pain." [42]

And then Hrothgar proceeds to apply the exemplum directly to Beowulf. The hero of the Geats, like Heremod, has been given great might by God and has used it successfully; happily, unlike Heremod, he has not been puffed up by his victories. But the danger of pride is always there. Any man who has great power and plenty may be tempted to pride.

> "Sometimes He [God] allows the spirit of a man of famous stock to wander in delight: gives him in his native land enjoyment of this world, a fencèd fortress of men to hold; makes regions of the world, a spacious empire, subject to him in such wise that in his folly he himself thinks it will never end. He lives in plenty; nothing—sickness nor old age—stands in his way. . . . All the world moves to his will. He knows no worse estate until a measure of overbearing pride waxes and grows in him, when the warder, the soul's guardian sleeps. That sleep is too sound, hedged in with cares: the slayer is very close, who from the winged bow shoots with evil intent. Then he is struck at the heart, under his armour, by the piercing arrow,—the crooked mysterious promptings of the accursed sprite. He cannot defend himself. What he had held for a long time seems to him too little. He covets, hostile in mind; never gives, in proud rejoicing, circlets overlaid with gold. No thought has he about the world to come, and he disdains the share of honours God, the Lord of Glory, gave him in time past." [43]

Beowulf now has power and riches, and the greater power of a king still awaits him. From the wealth of his own experience the humbled Hrothgar exhorts the young victor against the follies of pride. "Incline not to arrogance, famous warrior!" [44] Beowulf may think that he has the world at his feet. Hrothgar once thought so too. He had thought that the peace and happiness he had won for his people were to last forever; but they had been rudely shattered by the depradations of Grendel against which all his efforts had proved futile.

And what were Beowulf's reactions to this advice of the old king? He accepted it rejoicing; and, if we are to judge by the example that he set when he returned to his own country, he followed it closely. Like Hrothgar, he refused the kingship when it was offered him at the death of Hygelac; and, when in the course of events it came to him anyway, he conducted himself with such humble regard for the well-being of his subjects that they could say of him as they marched in song about his funeral mound that he was the mildest and the gentlest of men, and most kind to his people.[45] Beowulf's success did not make him arrogant, violent, or overbearing. In his last discourse, before the venom from the dragon silences him, he consoles himself in the recollection that he "did not pick treacherous quarrels." "In all this may I, [he says] sick with deadly wounds, have solace; because the Ruler of men may never charge me with the murder of kinsfolk when my life parts from my body." [46] And so Beowulf exemplifies to the end that virtue of humility which is the first check on the aberrated pursuit of honor.

And what about the second check, the virtue of charity? If it is possible, this permeates the action and motivation of the poem even more completely than humility. As we have seen, Beowulf was certainly not unaffected by the motive of personal honor, but it was to be won through the generous service of others. The chief motive for his actions in all three of the major episodes of the poem is the succor and welfare of others—of those who were not even his own countrymen in the first two episodes, and of his own subjects in the third episode. He knowingly risks his life in the first two episodes to save the Danes from the ravages of Grendel and his troll-mother; and in the last episode he sacrifices his very life to save his own people from the ravages of the dragon.

The poet leaves us with no possible room for doubt that charity is a prominent motive in the poem. The point is made explicit repeatedly by both Beowulf himself and by Hrothgar. When Beowulf heard about the terrible inroads of Grendel upon the subjects of Hrothgar, he "bade make ready for himself a good ship for the crossing of the waves,—said he would seek the warrior-king, the noted prince, over the swan's-road, since he was in need of men." [47] And he was seconded in his generous impulse by all his fellow wise Geats. They "did not blame him at all for the expedition, though he was dear to them; they urged on the stout-hearted one." [48] When he arrives at the court of the aged king, he announces that his reason for coming is the news he has received of Grendel's havoc in Heorot.

> "Grendel's doings became plainly known to me in my fatherland. Sea-farers say that this hall, this most noble build-ing, stands empty and useless to every man after the evening sun has become hidden under the vault of heaven. Then my people, the noble and wise men, advised me thus, lord Hroth-gar,—that I should visit thee, because they knew the strength of my might." [49]

Beowulf, it is clear, has come to help the Danes in their distress; and Hrothgar, in turn, recognizes that this is Beowulf's chief motive. "The holy God," he says, "has of his mercy sent him to us West-Danes, as I hope, to meet the terror of Grendel." [50] And to the hero himself he says: "My friend Beowulf, thou hast sought us to fight in our defence and for kindly aid." [51]

The motive of "kindly aid" comes to the fore again when Hrothgar is helpless in the face of the avengeful depradations of Grendel's mother. He admits that Beowulf alone can help his people in their distress. "Now once more is help to be had from thee alone." [52] And Beowulf again assures the troubled king that he is ready to succor him: "Sorrow not, wiseman. Better is it for each one of us that he should avenge his friend." [53] And with that Beowulf is off to avenge his friend Hrothgar for the loss of his counselor Aeschere—at the risk of his own life. When he plunges into the dreadful mere his thoughts are not of himself but of his followers, whom he entrusts to the care of the king should he see the end of his days in the struggle with the monster below.[54] And when triumphant and loaded with gifts from the grateful Hrothgar, he is making his farewell speech before departing for his home country, he makes an-

other generous offer of help, should the king be again beset by
his enemies.

> "If I learn this across the circuit of the sea,—that those
> around thy borders threaten harm, as enemies have done in
> times gone by, I'll bring a thousand thanes and heroes to thy
> help. As for Hygelac, lord of the Geats, I knew, though he is
> young, that he, his people's shepherd, will further me by
> word and deed, so that I may show my esteem for thee by
> deeds, and bring to thy rescue my shafted spear, the succor
> of my might, when thou hast need of men." [55]

Hrothgar is full of admiration for the ripe wisdom and generosity of the young hero: "The wise Lord put these speeches
in thy mind," he says, "never heard I a man talk more discreetly
at so young an age; strong art thou in thy might and ripe in
mind, wise in thy spoken words." [56]

The sage old king goes on to prophesy that this strength,
wisdom, and generosity will put Beowulf in line for a kingship
in his own land, where he will become the unselfish shepherd of
his people. And Beowulf does continue to show his unselfishness
upon arriving home by immediately turning over all the rich
treasure he had received from Hrothgar to his lord Hygelac,
and the jewels he had received from Queen Wealtheow to his
own Queen Hygde. Eventually, when the prophecy of Hrothgar comes true, Beowulf rules his people in peace for fifty years.
Then, like Hrothgar himself, "the veteran guardian of his people" is troubled by the ravages of the fire-breathing dragon.
True to form, Beowulf still shows himself to be the unselfish
guardian of his people and not only risks but loses his life to
free them from the disastrous visitations of the firedrake and
to win for them the treasure trove which the dragon guards.
When he has finally slain the monster, and sits dying from the
fatal wound he himself has received, and looks upon the great
hoard of treasure from the dragon's cave, he thanks God that
he has been allowed to win "such things for [his] people before
[his] death." [57] These are almost his final words:

"I utter in words my thanks to the ruler of all, the King of Glory, the everlasting Lord, for the treasures which I here gaze upon, in that I have been allowed to win such things for my people before my day of death! Now that I have given my old life in barter for the hoard of treasure, do ye henceforth supply the people's needs,—I may stay here no longer." [58]

So noteworthy has the life of Beowulf been in unselfish devotion to the needs of others in his youth and to those of his own people in his maturity and old age that he deserved the title of praise that was linked with his gentleness and mildness in his funeral hymn. "The people of the Geats . . . said that he had been of earthly kings the mildest and gentlest of men, the kindest to his people. . . ." [59] There can be little doubt, then, that service to others was a prominent motive in all the actions of Beowulf and one of his most endearing character- istics. He was, as we are also told in his funeral dirge, "most eager for fame," [60] but it was a fame, the whole action of the poem reveals, won in the generous and self-sacrificing service of others.

If any further evidence for the fact of Beowulf's spirit of Christian humility and charity is needed, it is provided by a comparison of his character with that of the noble Hrothgar and by a contrast with that of the less noble Unferth.

Hrothgar is pictured all through the first two episodes as a leader of great strength and courage and as a man of eminent virtue. He is represented as the entirely unselfish shepherd of his people, and hence as a king much loved and honored by them. When they are voicing their praise of Beowulf after his victory over Grendel, they are careful to make it clear that this praise is no reflection on the greatness of their own king.

Then Beowulf's exploit was proclaimed—many said that no other man, south or north, throughout the world, any- where on this vast earth, was more excellent among shield- bearers under the expanse of heaven, or worthier of empire.

> Yet did they not at all decry their friend and lord, the gracious Hrothgar; he was a good king.[61]

To his native prowess and moral uprightness, Hrothgar had added the wisdom of age and experience, and it is chiefly in this respect that he is contrasted with the young Beowulf throughout the earlier episodes of the poem. He acts as something of a Christian conscience for the youthful Beowulf and serves as a prototype for the mature and aging Beowulf of episode three.

Part of the unity of the whole poem is achieved by this resemblance of the mature Beowulf of episode three to the Hrothgar of episodes one and two. It is a relationship of type to prototype, and it appears that the *Beowulf* poet wishes us so to conceive it. The virtues which Hrothgar exemplifies so well in the first two episodes are exemplified to perfection by Beowulf in very similar circumstances in episode three. And the transition between the second and third episodes is achieved through the farewell speech of Hrothgar in which he urges Beowulf to learn by his experience and matured wisdom that the way to personal happiness and to peace and security for his future subjects is the way of humility, gentleness, and kindly service. Arrogance, violence, and selfishness, he warns Beowulf, can lead only to chaos and unhappiness for himself and his people.

And the life of Beowulf, the lord and protector of his people, is the life of Hrothgar all over again, except that it is raised to a higher degree of unselfishness in the surrender of his life for his people. The poet calls our attention to this parallel by emphasizing the fact of the identical fifty years of their respective reigns and by the advent of a monster to disturb the peace of their kingdoms in the late years of their reigns. These parallel situations make us almost unconsciously compare the characters of the two noble shepherds of their people. And when we do, we find that Hrothgar is himself pre-eminent in the virtues which he enjoins upon the youthful Beowulf and which that hero has already exemplified in the previous episodes and continues to exemplify in his maturity—the virtues of humble dependence upon God and unselfish service of his neighbor.

It is stated several times in the poem that Hrothgar is an accomplished warrior. But it is not in this that his true greatness consists. The virtues emphasized in the poem and for which his followers hold him in the greatest esteem are the same which elevate Beowulf to the level of a Christian hero—humility and charity. Hrothgar over and over again admits that in spite of the prowess and courage of himself and his followers they are helpless to rid themselves of the depradations of Grendel without the help of God.[62] He sees in Beowulf's advent a proffer of divine help and thanks God for the success of Beowulf's venture against both Grendel and his dam.[63] He is not ashamed to admit the superiority of Beowulf over himself and all the Danes; nor does he lose face with either the Danes or the Geats by this admission. For the true Christian the humble recognition of one's dependence upon God and the truth about oneself in relationship to others is ennobling and wins the generous respect rather than the contempt of others.

Hrothgar, moreover, is equally or perhaps even more characterized by a spirit of Christian charity. It is not without significance, in this connection, that the occasion of the ravages of Grendel was Hrothgar's construction of the mead hall, Heorot, for the shelter and entertainment of his people. The hateful monster was consumed with jealousy at the sound of the rejoicing in Heorot and determined to put an end to it by his murderous incursions, which soon emptied it of song and singers.[64] In this Grendel himself becomes the embodiment of the jealous hate which is diametrically opposed to the spirit of hospitality and unselfishness which had brought Heorot into being. It is not accidental that Hrothgar bears the title of protector of his people. Their welfare and safety have been his chief concern throughout his reign; and the greatest grief of his life has been his inability to rid them of the depradations of Grendel.[65] His great unselfish spirit is shown again in the generous gifts he bestows on Beowulf and his companions once the two monsters have been slain. Gift giving, of course, is one of the most common conventions of heroic sagas; but the kind of gift which Hrothgar gives reveals in a very special way the degree of his unselfishness. He gives Beowulf his own sword and horses—the two most prized possessions of any warrior.[66]

And in contrast to the unfeeling ruthlessness of some of Achilles' actions is the spirit of human gentleness that characterizes Hrothgar. This is nowhere more evident than in his speech of gratitude after Beowulf has slain Grendel, a speech in which he addresses Beowulf with all the tenderness of a loving father toward a son.[67] Gentleness, we recall, is a note that has a particularly Christian echo. It is a trait which makes the hero possessing it not only honored and respected but loved. It is a trait which we find not at all in Achilles and certainly not in a notable degree even in Aeneas. It is a heroic trait which only became prominent under the influence of what Chambers has called the "gentler virtues" of Christianity. The gentleness emphasized in both Hrothgar and Beowulf throughout the poem is all the more striking when we contrast it with the violence and the bloody kin-feuds that are frequently hinted at in the historical episodes and allusions, and which were far more characteristic of these Nordic peoples than the restraint and gentleness that pervade the *Beowulf* poem. Hrothgar's farewell advice to Beowulf to be humble, gentle, and kind toward his people carries all the more weight because his own practice has been such a good example of the virtues which he is preaching.

If Hrothgar, then, acts as a positive foil for the virtues of both the young and the mature Beowulf, Unferth certainly serves as a negative foil for them. He is in every respect inferior to Beowulf. He lacks his physical strength, his courage, and especially his moral integrity. In contrast to Hrothgar, he reacts with the typical jealousy of a small man to the obvious superiority of the Geatish hero. He tries to deflate Beowulf's reputation by reference to the Breca episode in the hero's past in which he was bested (so Unferth asserts) in a swimming contest. In contrast to the scathing wrath with which Achilles might be expected to meet such an envious thrust, Beowulf quite calmly recounts the true story which, without boastfulness, enhances his own reputation and quietly deflates Unferth's. And he also lays bare the truth of the present situation when he reminds Unferth of his own shady past as a murderer of his kin and of his present inability to cope with the destructive monster Grendel. The whole function of Unferth in the first two episodes, in fact, is to enhance the moral stature of Beowulf. Beowulf's very restraint in dealing with the unjust taunt of this jealous man disarms him and ultimately redeems him. Unferth gives him his own sword for the encounter with Grendel's dam; and, although it proves useless against the water troll, Beowulf returns it to its owner after the struggle with thanks and with no reference to its uselessness in the fight.[68] The significance of this situation is vastly strengthened by imagining the rejoinder that Achilles might have made in a like situation. The degree of Beowulf's unselfish magnanimity on this occasion is perhaps measured by the fact that, so far from carrying any grudge against Unferth for his jealousy and discourteous taunt on his arrival, he pays him an unsolicited compliment when he departs. Here Beowulf again shows himself to be the truly Christian magnanimous man who can overlook a slight to himself because he is interested in something bigger and more ennobling than his mere personal reputation. Beowulf is here totally unlike Achilles, who was willing to sacrifice the whole Greek army to reinstate his own personal honor in the eyes of the host.

One of the chief ways in which the barbaric pagan spirit showed itself among the Nordic races in general was in the family feuds which were constantly breaking out and resulting in murderous intrigues of all kinds. The new Christian doctrine of brotherly love, therefore, had a special significance for these Nordic peoples. The *Beowulf* poet seems to be weaving this part of the Christian message into the movement of his whole poem. In this connection, added significance is given to the fact that the monster Grendel is the offspring of the fratricidal Cain and that the ravages of the firedrake are occasioned by the theft of a fugitive from justice. Unferth is accused by Beowulf of having murdered his kin,[69] and there is a veiled reference to a future family feud in the household of Hrothgar that will wreck the peace which he has established.[70] One of the great sources of comfort to Beowulf at the end of his life is that he has not been guilty of murdering his own kin.[71] The many references to the instinct for such fratricidal feuds throughout the poem put us in touch with a very barbaric aspect of these Nordic races, indeed; but their presence gives greater point to the refining and civilizing influence of the new Christian ideal of gentleness and charity that is so admirably exemplified in both Hrothgar and Beowulf.

Another way in which the Christian spirit shows itself in the character of both Beowulf and Hrothgar is the role that war and prowess on the battlefield play in their careers. We hear references to many battles fought in the past in which they displayed their great prowess, but always we are given to understand that the battles were fought for the security and welfare of their peoples and not merely for the enhancement of their own personal reputations for strength and courage. In the story of Beowulf himself the poet was in a very different position from Virgil's in the matter of displaying his hero's battle prowess. Since Beowulf's antagonists were monsters explicitly identified with the powers of evil, the poet was under no necessity of glorifying the ordinary conflict in arms in which the hero is exalted by subduing a character like Hector or Turnus, who is almost as noble as, or nobler than, the conquering hero himself. In *Beowulf*, the emphasis is on the honor owing to the hero because of his humble dependence upon God for the might which enables him to overcome these monsters of evil, and for the unselfish generosity with which he dedicates his powers to the welfare of others. Since this was the main purpose of the poet, it is obvious why these legendary monsters as symbols of evil prove to be more appropriate adversaries for the hero than any mere historical or fictitious human adversary could ever be.[72] These legendary creatures and the conflict against them gain their true epic dignity and proportions not from their legendary background but from what those legends are made to symbolize. When the struggle of Beowulf against Grendel, the water troll, and the dragon are seen in this light, they take on more and not less dignity than the exploits of Odysseus against such preternatural creatures as Circe and Polyphemus. They have even a broader import than the battlings of Aeneas to found a new Troy because they suggest the broader struggle of every man to found a spiritual kingdom safe from the incursions of the powers of darkness.

This discussion, then, should make apparent that the character of Beowulf is such a complete verification of the Christian notion of the heroic or the magnanimous that it would almost seem to have been created to exemplify the virtue as Saint Paul and the early church Fathers sketched it—limited by the virtues of humility and charity. One can hardly read *Beowulf* with a knowledge of this ideal in mind without recognizing that the author has assimilated that new ideal completely and made it a guiding principle in his creation of the two chief characters in the poem as well as in the ordering and motivation of all three of the major episodes. If you remove from the poem all that this spirit has given it, practically nothing of the body of the poem remains. Reading *Beowulf* in the light which the Christian notion of magnanimity throws upon it strengthens immeasurably the conclusion of Frederick Klaeber that

> the Christian elements are almost without exception so deeply ingrained in the very fabric of the poem that they cannot be explained away as the work of a reviser or later interpolator. In addition, it is instructive to note that whilst the [historical] episodes are all but free from those modern influences, the main story has been thoroughly imbued with the spirit of Christianity.[73]

NOTES

[1] For the most part, the multiple-authorship theory as it affected *Beowulf* was a by-product of the German scholarship which made the poem out to be a perfect example of a particular theory of the folk-epic. Klaeber summarizes the chief theories of these critics in the introduction to his edition of the poem (pp. cii-cvii). In his concluding remarks on this school of criticism, he has this to say: "That the Christian elements have not been merely grafted on the text, but are most intimately connected with the very substance of the poem has been remarked before. A certain want of harmony that has resulted from the Christian presentation of heathen material is not such as to warrant the assumption that a professed redactor went over a previously existing version, revising it by interpolation or substitution of Christian touches. The mere technical difficulties of such a process would have been of the greatest and vestiges of imperfect suture would be expected to be visible in more than one passage of our text. No serious differences of language, diction, or meter can be adduced in favor of multiple authorship."—Frederick Klaeber, *Beowulf and the Fight at Finnsburg* (Boston: D. C. Heath and Company, 1950), p. civ. Reprinted by permission of the publisher.

[2] *Ibid.*, pp. xlix-l.

[3] R. W. Chambers, *Beowulf: An Introduction to the Study of the Poem with a Discussion of the Stories of Offa and Finn* (Cambridge: Cambridge University Press, 1932), p. 126. Reprinted by permission of the publishers.

[4] *Ibid.*, p. 128.

[5] R. W. Chambers, "*Beowulf* and the 'Heroic Age' in England," *Man's Unconquerable Mind* (Philadelphia: Albert Saifer, 1953), p. 65.

[6] Charles W. Kennedy, *Beowulf, The Oldest English Epic* (New York: Oxford University Press, 1940), p. xlix.

[7] *Ibid.*, p. l.

[8] Clark Hall, *Beowulf and the Finnesburg Fragment a Translation into Modern English Prose*, newly edited and revised by C. L. Wrenn (London: George Allen & Unwin Ltd., 1950), pp. 32-33 [247]. All references to Beowulf, unless otherwise indicated, will

be to this translation. The references will be made under the translator's name, Hall. In each reference to the poem the number in
brackets following the reference refers to the first line of the quotation in the original Old English edition of Frederick Klaeber.

⁹ *Ibid.*, p. 38 [369].

¹⁰ *Ibid.*, p. 148 [2538].

¹¹ *Ibid.*, p. 177 [3182]. *Lofgeornost* is the phrase in the original,
and *lof* in Old English does not merely mean praise but the kind
of glory or external recognition that was particularly suited to the
man of exploits.

¹² *Ibid.*, p. 37 [338]. *For wlenco* is well rendered by the phrase
"from prowess"; *for higeþrymmum* comes close to being the Old
English equivalent for magnanimity or high-spiritedness. Together
the two phrases seem to put the emphasis here on a courageous
display of physical prowess. But simple unselfish nobleness of spirit
is not entirely ruled out of the context because the herald remarks
that it is not sanctuary for himself as an exile that brings Beowulf
hither, *nalles for wræcsiðum*.

¹³ *Ibid.*, pp. 41-42 [406].

¹⁴ *Ibid.*, p. 53 [636]. *Eorlic ellen*—the courage of a hero. *Ellen*
can mean strength or courage; but whichever way it is rendered
here, it savors of the kind of prowess associated with the old
heroic ideal.

¹⁵ *Ibid.*, p. 54 [658]. *Gemyne mærþo, mægenellen cyð*—are
Hrothgar's words. *Mærðo* can mean glorious deeds or the fame
that comes from them; in either case Hrothgar is bidding Beowulf
be mindful of his reputation. The phrase *mægenellen cyð*—rendered literally, "make known thy mighty valor"—definitely invites Beowulf to the kind of deeds that will win him fame.

¹⁶ *Ibid.*, p. 62 [818]. *Guðhreð gyfeþe. Hreð* is another Old
English word for glory or triumph, and compounded with *guð* it
means "glory in battle." The almost innumerable synonyms for the
idea of glory won in battle in Old English in itself suggests the old
heroic tradition in which this value was so much in the foreground.

¹⁷ *Ibid.*, p. 91 [1386]. *Wyrce sē þe mōte dōmes ǣr dēaþe.*
In the phrase, *Wyrce sē dōmes*, "let him endeavor to win glory,"
we have still another synonym for glory. *Dom* primarily means a
judgment or decree; but, in this and several other places in the
poem, it means the judgment cast on the hero's deeds of valor, or

the recognition of his achievement, which is a periphrasis for glory.

[18] *Ibid.*, p. 98 [1534]. The word for glory here is again *lof*—*longsumme lof*—which Hall renders as "enduring fame."

[19] *Ibid.*, p. 147 [2513]. The phrase employed here is *fæhðe sēcan mǣrðu fremman.* Hall translates it "seek combat and get renown." It might more literally be rendered—"seek battle and do glorious deeds." But since, as we have remarked before, *mǣrðo* means both fame and the glorious deeds upon which it is based, Hall's freer translation is justified and does not substantially alter the sense of the passage. Beowulf *is* seeking his own fame in the battle.

[20] *Ibid.*, p. 154 [2677].

[21] J. R. R. Tolkien, in his admirable essay "Beowulf: The Monsters and the Critics," in which he does so much to rescue *Beowulf* as a poem from its fate at the hands of many nonliterary critics, still interprets the character of Beowulf himself as substantially pagan in his attitude toward honor: "When we make allowance for imperfections of execution, and even for some intentional modification of character in old age (when Beowulf becomes not unnaturally much more like Hrothgar), it is plain that the characters and sentiments of the two chief actors in the poem are differently conceived and drawn. Where Beowulf's thoughts are revealed by the poet we can observe that his real trust was *in his own might.*" —*Proceedings of the British Academy*, XXII (1936), 286-287. It is Professor Tolkien's contention throughout this essay that it was the intention of the *Beowulf* poet, himself a Christian and well acquainted with Anglo-Saxon poetry that had Christianized the old pagan lays, to create in the character of Beowulf a noble hero of the old pagan stamp and to contrast him with Hrothgar, who was conceived along more Christian lines. As stimulating and constructive as Professor Tolkien's whole discussion of *Beowulf* is in the matter of the structure of the poem, and as hesitant as I am to quarrel with an interpretation of a scholar as eminent as Professor Tolkien in this field, I cannot agree with him that in the character of Beowulf the poet was attempting to portray an essentially pagan hero. I hope that the discussion in the text of this chapter will make clear the reasons for my own opinion in the matter.

22 "After that the people of the Geats went quickly up on dry land; they made fast the ship; their coats of mail, their armour, rang; they thanked God that for them the sea-paths had been easy." —Hall, p. 31 [227]. *Gode þancedon* is the term employed in the original. Tolkien (*op. cit.*) tries to make a great deal of the fact that we more often hear the poet commenting on Beowulf's recognition of his dependence upon God than we hear Beowulf himself explicitly acknowledging it. But the fact remains that on several important occasions Beowulf does acknowledge it, and on numerous other occasions the poet calls attention to the fact of this dependence—one of the facts which man needed revelation to clarify for him.

23 *ðǣr gelȳfan sceal/Dryhtnes dōme sē þe hine dēað nimeð* [440]. *Dryhtnes dōme* "judgment of the Lord." This is not the same thing as resigning oneself to the blind dictates of fate, but sounds much more like the acknowledgment of a knowing and providential Lord and Master; and these words are on the lips of Beowulf, not the Beowulf poet. It is true that Beowulf ends this very speech with the words: "*Gǣð ā wyrd swā hio scel!*" [455]. But such residuary fatalistic expressions here and elsewhere do not negate the whole tenor of Beowulf's own actions and of the movement of the poem as a whole—which all add up to an impressive insistence upon man's dependence upon God for all his achievements.

24 The original reads: *Hūru Gēata lēod georne truwode/mōdgan mægnes, metodes hyldo.* Hall translates this: "Indeed the chief of the Geats trusted firmly in his proud might, and in the favour of the Creator."—*Op. cit.*, p. 55. Tolkien correctly points out that there is no "and" in the original and that there should be none in the translation. The poet is speaking here and acknowledging that Beowulf's proud might is a favor from the Creator— the *mōdgan mægnes* is *metodes hyldo*—an eminently Christian way of looking at it. It is true that the poet is not here saying that Beowulf himself looks at it in this light, but since Beowulf says as much elsewhere in the poem, that is irrelevant.

25 Hall, p. 55 [686]. "*Ond siþðan witig God/on swā hwæ-þere hond hālig Dryhten/mǣrðo dēme, swā him gemet þince.*" "*Witig God*" and "*hālig Dryhten.*" The wise God and the Holy

Lord do not seem to be terms suitable to the lips of a character whom the poet, in Tolkien's contention, has conceived on the old pagan pattern.

[26]*Ibid.*, p. 56 [696].

[27] *Ibid.*, p. 69 [966]. The term for God used by Beowulf here is *Metod*, a word, it is true, which in old Germanic languages was employed for the decrees of Fate, but the term here and at the end of Beowulf's speech [979] has much more of the connotation of the judgment of a personal God.

[28] *Ibid.*, p. 69 [977].

"*ðǣr ābidan sceal maga māne fāh miclan dōmes, hū him scīr Metod scrīfan wille.*" Here *Metod* is employed again by Beowulf; but it can hardly be translated in its context as merely the decrees of Fate. It is much more personal than that; and even if *scīr Metod* is not translated as "glorious Creator" with Hall, "how the glorious Lord will sentence him" is the minimum meaning that can be given the passage. This still expresses the idea of a personal God and not mere impersonal Fate.

[29] *Ibid.*, p. 85 [1270]. Here the terms used for God are *God* (1271) and *Anwaldan* [1272], "ruler." The poet is not only observing in his own person here that Beowulf's might was from God, but he says that Beowulf himself acknowledged the fact and relied on the help and grace of God to enable him to overcome the fiend: "*ond him tō Anwaldan āre gelȳfde,/frōfre ond fultum; ðȳ hē þone fēond ofercwōm, gehnǣgde helle gāst.*"

[30] *Ibid.*, p. 99 [1550].

[31] *Ibid.*, p. 105 [1657]. In this instance Beowulf himself uses not *Metod* but *God* in his acknowledgment of divine help in his struggle: *ætrihte wæs/gūð getwǣfed, nymðe mec God scylde.*

[32] *Ibid.*, p. 131 [2182].

[33] *Ibid.*, p. 160 [2794]. "*Ic ðāra frætwa Frēan ealles ðanc,/ Wuldercyninge wordum secge,/ēcum Dryhtne, þē ic hēr on starie.*" The terms *Frēan ealles*—Ruler of all—and *Wuldercyninge* —King of Glory—are perfectly appropriate for the one providential God of Christian revelation with almost an Old Testament overtone to them.

[34] *Ibid.*, p. 163 [2874].

[35] *Ibid.*, p. 163 [2854].

[36] *Ibid.*, p. 39 [381].

[37] *Ibid.*, p. 44 [478].

[38] *Ibid.*, pp. 67-68 [928].

[39] *Ibid.*, p. 68 [946].

[40] *Ibid.*, p. 107 [1704].

[41] Klaeber makes the following comment on this farewell speech of Hrothgar: "The much discussed harangue of Hrothgar, which shows the moralizing, didactic turn of the poem at its very height, falls into four well-marked divisions, viz. a. 1700-9^a; b. 1709^b-24^a (the second Heremod digression); c. 1724^b-68 (the 'sermon' proper); d. 1769-84. It is conspicuous for the blending of heroic and theological motives. There can be no doubt that this address of the king's forms an organic element in the structural plan of the epic, corresponding in its function to the Hrothgar speech after the first combat together with the first Heremod episode. Moreover, it is entirely in harmony with the high moral tone, the serious outlook, and spiritual refinement of the poem. Of course, its excessive length and strong homiletic flavor have laid the third division, and even other parts, open to the charge of having been interpolated by a man versed and interested in theology, and it is, indeed, possible that the 'sermon' represents a later addition to the text."—*Op. cit.*, p. 190. But interpolated or not, the "sermon" does not contain anything that is out of harmony with the characters of either Hrothgar or Beowulf as their previous actions in the poem have revealed them to us. It might be interesting to compare the road to pride as it is outlined in Hrothgar's speech here and as it is treated in Saint Ignatius' meditation on *The Two Standards*, in his *Spiritual Exercises*. The progression through love of riches, to power, to pride, and then to all other vices is the same in both.

[42] Hall, p. 108 [1716].

[43] *Ibid.*, pp. 108-109 [1728].

[44] *Ibid.*, p. 110 [1760].

[45] *Ibid.*, p. 177 [3180].

[46] *Ibid.*, p. 157 [2740]. It is worth remarking here that the effect of the new Christian spirit of gentleness as it is revealed in the character of Beowulf is strengthened when we contrast him with the many kin-murderers that are hinted at in the historical digressions in the poem. These flashes of the background out of which Beowulf emerged makes all the more glorious and Christian his

dying boast that he thanks God that he can never be accused of having taken false oaths or of murdering his kin.

47 *Ibid.*, p. 30 [198].

48 *Ibid.*, p. 30 [202].

49 *Ibid.*, p. 41 [409].

50 *Ibid.*, p. 39 [381].

51 *Ibid.*, p. 43 [458]. Klaeber says of this aspect of Beowulf's character: "In his role as a deliverer from the ravages of the monsters he might well be likened to ancient heroes like Hercules and Theseus. With all the heroic attributes the poet has conferred on him, the dominant trait of the hero is his wonderful eagerness to help others."—*Op. cit.*, p. li.

52 *Ibid.*, p. 90 [1376].

53 *Ibid.*, p. 91 [1384].

54 See [1475-1490].

55 Hall, p. 113 [1826].

56 *Ibid.*, p. 114 [1840].

57 *Ibid.*, p. 160 [2797].

58 *Ibid.*, p. 160 [2794].

59 *Ibid.*, p. 177 [3180].

60 *Ibid.* [3182].

61 *Ibid.*, p. 64 [856].

62 *Ibid.*, p. 30 [190]; p. 44 [475].

63 These are Hrothgar's words as he looks at Grendel's hand in the hall of Heorot: "For this sight let thanksgiving rise at once to the Almighty! Many horrors and afflictions have I endured through Grendel: yet God, the King of Glory, can ever work wonder on wonder. It was but now that I despaired of ever seeing a remedy for any of my troubles. . . . Now through the might of the Lord, a warrior has done a deed which up to now we all could not accomplish by our schemings."—*Ibid.*, pp. 67-68 [927].

64 "Then the mighty spirit who dwelt in darkness bore grievously a time of hardship, in that he heard each day loud revelry in hall;—there was the sound of the harp, the clear song of the minstrel."—*Ibid.*, p. 24 [87].

65 *Ibid.*, pp. 110-111 [1774].

66 *Ibid.*, pp. 72-73 [1020].

67 "Now, Beowulf, best of men, in my heart will I love thee as a son; henceforth keep well this new kinship."—*Ibid.*, p. 68 [947].

68 *Ibid.*, p. 112 [1807].

69 *Ibid.*, p. 50 [587].

70 *Ibid.*, p. 176 [3150].

71 "In all this may I, sick with deadly wounds, have solace, because the Ruler of men may never charge me with the murder of kinsfolk when my life parts from my body."—*Ibid.*, p. 157 [2740].

72 Professor Tolkien, in the essay previously cited—"Beowulf: The Monsters and the Critics"—insists on the artistic rightness of the *Beowulf* poet's making the fight with the monsters the central conflict of his story rather than any battling with historical figures, all of which are relegated to the historical episodes. Although I disagree with Professor Tolkien's interpretation of the character of Beowulf, I am in complete accord with his insistence on the essential rightness of centering the story of Beowulf on the conflict with monsters. No battle with any mere human adversary could ever be given the universal and symbolical significance that the fight with Grendel, the water-troll, and the dragon inevitably have in this poem even for a modern reader. Such broader significance would probably have been even more inevitable for the audience for which the poem was written.

73 Klaeber, *op. cit.*, p. l.

CHAPTER SEVEN

Magnanimity in Saint Augustine and Saint Thomas Aquinas

"Wherefore without doubt, we had better resist this desire [for honor] than yield to it. For so much the nearer are we to God, as we are purer from this impurity: which although in this life it be not fully rooted out of the heart, because it is a temptation that troubles even the most proficient in religion, yet let the love of righteousness suppress the thirst of ambitiousness. . . . But the others, living in an earthly city, wherein the end of all their endeavours was by themselves propounded to themselves, the fame and domination of this world and not the eternity of heaven; not in the everlasting life, but in their own ends, and the mouths of their posterity: what should they love, but glory, whereby they desired to survive after death in the memories and mouths of such as commended them."

SAINT AUGUSTINE: *The City of God*,
Book V, Chapter 14

"Honour denotes reverence shown to a person in witness of his excellence. Now two things have to be considered with regard to man's honour. The first is that a man has not from himself the thing in which he excels, for this is, as it were, something Divine in him, wherefore on this count honour is due principally, not to him but to God. The second point that calls for observation is that the thing in which man excels is given to him by God, that he may profit

others thereby: wherefore a man ought so far to be
pleased that others bear witness to his excellence, as
this enables him to profit others."
SAINT THOMAS AQUINAS: Summa Theologica,
IIa, IIae, CXXXI, articulus 1, ad corpus

The concept of magnanimity as it unfolds in the writings of
the Venerable Bede and the *Beowulf* remains recognizably like
the ideal of Christian practice expounded by Saint Paul in his
Epistles to the Corinthians. As the Christian consciousness matured, however, there arose a very discernible split in the attitude toward what was rational and Christian in the pursuit of
honor. This split is perhaps best revealed by an examination of
some of the remarks of Saint Augustine and Saint Thomas
Aquinas on the subject.

The matrix of much of Saint Augustine's thought was Platonic philosophy. Contrary to the Aristotelian view, the pursuit
of honor had been given a very subordinate position in Plato's
tripartite division of the human soul. We will recall that for
Plato each of the three parts of the human soul had its own specific drive and object. The object of the lowest part was sense
pleasure; that of the middle or spirited part was honor; while
the object of the highest or rational part was knowledge and
wisdom.[1] For the well-being of the individual it was necessary
that the drive for honor and pleasure be rigidly controlled and
directed by the rational power of the soul. And what was true
of the individual was true also of men in society because for
Plato there was a correspondence between the division of the
soul in the individual and the division of classes in society. The
drive of the unenlightened lower classes was for pleasure; that
of the middle or guardian, warrior class was for honor; while
the philosophers, the only truly enlightened class in Plato's
hierarchy, were dedicated to a knowledge of the eternal ideas.[2]
For the well-being of society, then, the guardians' pursuit of

honor and the populace's pursuit of pleasure had to be directed and controlled by the philosophers. It was Saint Augustine's absorption of the Platonic view of reality, suspicious of the whole sense world as once removed from the real world of ideas, and his many years of addiction to the Manichaean idea that everything material was intrinsically evil that partly conditioned and colored his own view of reality and of the whole question of worldly honor in particular.

One of the most fundamental postulates of Saint Augustine's whole interpretation of history is his distinction between the two Cities—the City of God and the City of Man. The inhabitants of both Cities are dedicated to the pursuit of glory but glory of very different kinds:

> Two loves therefore have given origin to these two cities, self-love in contempt of God unto the earthly, love of God in contempt of one's self to the heavenly. The first seeks the glory of men, and the latter desires God only as the testimony of the conscience, the greatest glory. That glories in itself, and this in God. That exalts itself in self-glory: this says to God: "My glory and the lifter up of my head." That boasts of the ambitious conquerors led by the lust of sovereignty: in this all serve each other in charity, both the rulers in counselling and the subjects in obeying. That loves worldly virtue in the potentates: this says unto God: "I will love Thee, O Lord, My strength." [3]

Here the dichotomy between the pursuits of the two Cities seems to be severe and irreconcilable. And elsewhere the opposition between the two pursuits seems equally sharp. Of the inhabitants of the earthly City he says in another place:

> But the others living in an earthly city, wherein the end of all their endeavours was by themselves propounded to themselves, the fame and domination of this world and not the eternity of heaven; not in the everlasting life, but in their

own ends, and the mouths of their posterity: what should they love, but glory, whereby they desired to survive after death in the memories and mouths of such as commended them.—I, p. 163.

Saint Augustine does concede that members of the City of God may be recognized for their achievement, but, despising the honor of working for the glory of God and men, they transmit all the recognition they receive to the glory of God:

And when this divine life, conversation, and doctrine of theirs [of the Apostles] having suppressed all hardness of heart, and erected the peace of righteousness, was crowned with an unbounded glory in Christ's Church; in this did not they rest, as in the expected guerdon of their virtues, but referred it all to Christ's glory, by whose grace they were what they were. And the same did they transfuse into such as they converted unto the love of Him, whereby they might become such as they were before them: for to keep them from touch of human ambition their Master taught them thus: "Take heed that you do not your good deeds before men, to be seen of them, or else ye shall have no reward of your Father which is in heaven." But lest they should mis-conceive this, and fear to do well before men; and so become less profitable by striving to keep their virtuous acts in secret, than otherwise; He says again: "Let your light so shine before men, that they may see your good works and glorify your Father which is in Heaven." Do not well with an intent that men should see you do so, and so turn to behold you, who by yourselves are nothing: but do so that they may glorify your Father in heaven unto whom if they turn they may be such as you are.—I, pp. 162-163.

This is a precise and very severe interpretation of the Pauline ideal.

In another place Saint Augustine concedes that among the pagans some good was achieved out of a motivation of earthly glory and that even a Christian, though not holy, might be less base in acting from this rather than from an even less worthy motive.

> Those that do not bridle their exorbitant desires by faith, by the power of the Holy Spirit, and the love of that intellectual beauty, though they cannot be holy, yet they may be less base, because of their love of human glory. Tully could not dissemble this, in his book *Of the Commonwealth*, where speaking of the education of a prince for a city, he says, "he must be nourished with glory"; and so thereupon infers what worthy deeds this glory had drawn from his ancestors. So that they were so far from resisting this vice, that they did wholly give themselves to augment and excite it, thinking it useful to the State.—I, p. 161.

But whatever concessions he is willing to make about this motive of action among the pagan Romans, Saint Augustine is insistent that it is an unworthy motive for Christian action.

> Wherefore without doubt, we had better resist this desire [for earthly fame] than yield to it. For so much the nearer are we to God, as we are purer from this impurity: which although in this life it be not fully rooted out of our heart, because it is a temptation that troubles even the most proficient in religion, yet let the love of righteousness suppress the thirst of ambitiousness. And thus if some things be unrespected because men approve them not, and yet be good and honest; then let the love of human praise blush and give place to the love of truth. For this is a great enemy of our faith, if the desire of glory have more room in our hearts than the fear of God; and therefore He says: "How can you believe that expect honour one from another and seek not the honour that cometh of God?"—I, p. 162.

The only use to which Saint Augustine can see the members of the City of God putting the pursuit of honor by the members of the Earthly City is as an example of dedication and diligence.

Let us consider what obstacles these men have scorned, what pains they have taken, what desires they have suppressed, and only for this human glory which afterwards they received as the reward of their virtues; and let this serve to suppress our pride also, that seeing the city wherein we are promised habitation and kingdom is as far different from this in excellence as heaven from earth, life eternal from mirth temporal, firm glory from fuming vainglory, angels' company from men's, and His light that made the sun and moon from the light of the sun and moon; we may feel that the citizens of this heavenly region have done just nothing for attaining this celestial dwelling, seeing that the others have taken such pains in that habitation of earth which they had already attained.—I, p. 165.

This is admittedly a very severe and rather chilling view of the whole sphere of earthly pursuits and one that is almost infinitely removed from the exaggeration of personal honor in the Aristotelian analysis of magnanimity. It is a view which sees no possibility of compromise between the pursuit of temporal glory in the Earthly City and the pursuit of eternal glory in the City of God.

But not all Christian philosophers took this rigid a view, as even a brief analysis of Saint Thomas Aquinas' discussion of magnanimity will show. As a matter of fact, here as in so many other instances, what Saint Thomas has to say is the result of an attempt to synthesize the Aristotelian analyses with the truths of Christian revelation. But here as elsewhere, too, as reliant as he is on Aristotle for terms and the structuring of his thought, the reality of magnanimity as he defines it turns out to be something vastly different from the virtue as Aristotle had sketched it.

Thomas agrees with Aristotle that magnanimity is a virtue dealing with the right-reasoned attitude toward honor;[4] and he agrees, too, that it is concerned with the great honors[5] owing to a great man who is really pre-eminent in all the virtues. Thomas, like Aristotle, speaks of two virtues dealing with honor

—one nameless and dealing with the ordinary honors owing to the ordinary man and another dealing with the great honors owing to the man who is truly extraordinary. The latter is the virtue of magnanimity.

> We must conclude that the proper matter of magnanimity is great honour, and that a magnanimous man tends to such things as are deserving of honour.[6]

The wording here is important. It suggests that for Saint Thomas, the magnanimous man should be more concerned with the great deeds that deserve honor than with the honor that accrues to them. The good deeds are the end of his endeavor; the honor is only the natural consequences of the end achieved; and about the latter the magnanimous man, says Saint Thomas,[7] conducts himself according to reason.

From the very outset of his discussion of magnanimity Saint Thomas is careful to reconcile it with humility. There is no conflict between humility and magnanimity; they are, rather, necessary concomitants in a great man who looks at himself truthfully:

> There is in man something great which he possesses through the gift of God; and something defective which accrues to him through the weakness of nature. Accordingly magnanimity makes a man deem himself worthy of great things in consideration of the gifts he holds from God: thus if his soul is endowed with great virtue, magnanimity makes him tend to perfect works of virtue; and the same is to be said of the use of any other good, such as science or external fortune. On the other hand, humility makes a man think little of himself in consideration of his own deficiency, and magnanimity makes him despise others in so far as they fall away from God's gifts: since he does not think so much of others as to do anything wrong for their sake. Yet humility makes us honour others and esteem them better than ourselves, in so far as we see some of God's gifts in them.[8]

Here Saint Thomas is introducing a very effective moderator into the attitude to be assumed toward honor. If a man keeps in mind the fact that whatever good he has he has from God, he must, if he is rational, recognize that it is God rather than himself who deserves the honor. If he further bears in mind that whatever evil there is in him comes entirely from himself, he must also recognize that of himself he deserves dishonor rather than honor. Any great gifts, then, whether they are virtues, riches, knowledge, or power, should engender in their possessor not the desire for great honor but rather the desire to do great things, to put these gifts to the best possible use for God and for his neighbor. Honor, again, should not be the end of his action, although it will be a natural consequence of it. And as a matter of fact, right-minded men, seeing his good works and recognizing that his powers for doing them are gifts of God, will glorify God for them rather than him. That is what Christ was advocating when He said: "So let your light shine before men, that they may see your good works and glorify [not you but] your Father who is in heaven" (Matt. 5:16). This is admittedly a very exalted, unselfish ideal, and one not very often realized even by Christians; but the point here is that it *is* the ideal held up by Christ, by His Apostles, and by Christian philosophers in all ages. From it the selfishness, so obtrusive in Aristotle's discussion of the magnanimous man, has entirely disappeared.

The desire of the magnanimous man to do great things for God and his neighbor, to realize to their fullest the gifts God has given him, is quite consonant with a recognition that in himself and left to himself he has many weaknesses and sinful tendencies. This double condition within himself, of good and bad, of strength and weakness, also affects his attitude toward his fellow men. And here again the basis of Saint Thomas' observations is quite different from Aristotle's on the same subject. The magnanimous man does not despise or contemn his fellow men who have received fewer gifts from God than he has, but only evil men who have not made use of the gifts God has given them. And even them he despises only to the extent that he will not allow them to induce him to do evil. On the other hand, he admires good men because he sees that they have made use of the gifts that God has given them. All of this, it must be admitted, is a very realistic check upon man's pride and tendency to contemn or despise others.

Contrary to the opinion of Aristotle that the magnanimous man is incapable of excess in his claims for honor, Saint Thomas holds that presumption, ambition, and vanity are all excesses against the virtue of magnanimity.[9] Presumption—the endeavor to do things beyond one's capacities—is, by definition, the excess of the mediocre man who strives to do great things only compatible with the powers of the really great man. But in the Christian economy, even the magnanimous man can become presumptuous by forgetting that, without the grace of God, he can do nothing in the supernatural order. Saint Thomas does not emphasize this point in his discussion of presumption, but actually it is a consideration that can keep even the greatest man humble in the realization of his complete dependence upon God for any achievement in the supernatural order.

What Saint Thomas says about ambition is more immediately pertinent to the subject of this chapter because ambition is concerned directly with a man's attitude toward honor. Ambition is defined as an irrational desire for honor.[10] The desire for honor, Saint Thomas observes, can be irrational in three ways:

> First, when a man desires recognition of an excellence which he has not: this is to desire more than his share of honour. Secondly, when a man desires honour for himself without referring it to God. Thirdly, when a man's appetite rests in honour itself, without referring it to the profit of others.[11]

The first aberration is again the excess of the mediocre man against magnanimity—the desire of honor for excellences which he actually does not possess. But the last two aberrations the magnanimous man himself may also be guilty of. His very eminence may tempt him to forget his dependence upon God for all that he is and has and his obligation to employ these gifts for the benefit of his neighbor and not merely for his own honor and glory. Becoming irrational, then, in his attitude toward honor, he really ceases to be the genuinely magnanimous man and becomes the ambitious one. Saint Thomas reiterates these two limitations on a great man's attitude toward honor so often that there can be no possible doubt about the importance he placed upon them as marks of the true Christian view of honor. They make the Christian virtues of humility and charity clear norms for judging the rationality of a great man's attitude toward the great honors that *are* his due.

The same two points are emphasized again in Saint Thomas' discussion of the third excess against magnanimity—vainglory. Glory, or the clear, public recognition of one's excellence, is in itself neither evil nor opposed to magnanimity, but vainglory is. Glory, according to Thomas, can be vain in three ways: first, when one seeks it for something that is not worth public recognition; second, when one seeks it from those whose judgment is not reliable; and third, when the person seeking the glory fails to refer his glory to God's honor or the spiritual welfare of his neighbor but seeks it for his own satisfaction alone.[12] In the third, we are reminded again of the double rein that should hold in check the Christian's desire for honor and glory. In this connection it is pertinent to compare the proper attitude of the magnanimous man toward glory with the attitude which God Himself takes toward His own glory. God did not create the world in order to receive the recognition, the honor, and the glory of men. As an infinitely perfect being, God had no need of such recognition, and could have had no such selfish motive in creation. If He created at all, it had to be in order to manifest and communicate His perfection to someone outside Himself. Rational creatures, seeing the excellence of God manifested in His creatures, do acknowledge it, do honor and glorify God;

but that was not the motive for which God created. The case of the magnanimous man should be like that of God.[13] His chief concern should be great deeds done with God's help for his fellow men. Men, seeing these deeds, will acknowledge them; they will glorify the doer and God through Whose gifts they were made possible. But the glory should not be the sole motive of the magnanimous man, any more than glory was the motive of God in creating.[14]

If the two conditions reiterated so often by Saint Thomas are fulfilled, a man may seek his own honor and glory; in fact, he may on occasion be obliged to do so for the greater glory of God and the benefit of his neighbor. Men in high positions of trust, for example, cannot be indifferent about their reputations; but they should secure them, of course, by performing the duties of their positions in such a way as to merit honor and glory.

Like Aristotle, Saint Thomas admits that a great man may, out of ignorance of his own abilities or from fear of failure, become guilty of pusillanimity by not doing the great things of which he is actually capable.[15] But the repeated cautions that he gives the great man about his attitude toward honor suggests that to him the far more dangerous aberration from magnanimity is by excess rather than by defect. To him ambition and vanity are greater pitfalls than pusillanimity. Vanity he makes one of the cardinal vices,[16] allied to pride, which he considers the root of all vice. This attitude is a great remove from that of Aristotle, whose definition of magnanimity, the crown of all his virtues, is hardly distinguishable from pride which Saint Thomas makes the queen of all vices.[17]

Of the two views of honor represented here by Saint Augustine and Saint Thomas Aquinas, it was the severer view of Saint Augustine that more generally prevailed in the writings of the Middle Ages. Earthly honor and fame are more often than not looked on with suspicion by medieval writers. In Chaucer's *The House of Fame*, for example, Dame Fame is represented as the plaything of Fickle Fortune, and her palace is built on ice. Her decisions are not based on man's virtues but are made quite arbitrarily through the golden trumpet of "Clere Laude" or the black trumpet of "Sklaundre." [18] We are under no illusion, of course, that medieval man in general was very much different from any other man in his attitude toward honor, place, and position. In fact, we have the definite impression that medieval moralists and poets felt constantly compelled to bring their readers around to see the alluring reality of personal honor and fame *sub specie aeternitatis*. This partly explains the peculiar concept of tragedy that came to prevail in the Middle Ages, the spectacle of great men whose fall from the heights was as certain as their rise to worldly greatness because they were strapped to the fickle wheel of fortune. This ubiquitous medieval theme, still being expressed in such works as Boccaccio's *De Casibus Virorum Illustrium*, Chaucer's *Monk's Tale*, and Lydgate's *Mirror for Magistrates*, aimed at discrediting earthly honor or fame as a dominant aim and strove to turn men's minds to heavenly glory as a final and lasting end in life.

But when we come to the Renaissance, especially to the Renaissance in Italy, all this changes radically. A fresh study of pagan literature, especially of Greek literature, in which the sense of personal glory played such an important part, a tremendous upsurge of creativity in all the arts, the beginnings of scientific inquiry which radically changed men's concept of the physical universe, the adventuresome explorations that suddenly expanded the globe on which men lived, the growing sense of a national self-consciousness, and the invention of printing—these are only some of the most important developments that focused man's attention on his own potentialities for greatness and seemed to make achievement and consequent glory on this earth almost limitless and far more appealing than the remote glory of heaven. It was natural, then, that, in these circumstances, the pursuit of personal fame, honor, and glory became a predominant passion of Renaissance man.

Whether we study Italian Renaissance history, poetry, or art, we are constantly given the impression that Italy is going through a new adolescence in which everything is subordinated to personal honor and fame. In politics the drive ends in the absolutist tendencies observed and recorded by Machiavelli in his *Il Principe*. In the art world we have the same drive culminating in the ideal of the *l'uomo universale*, which came so near fulfillment in the titanic achievements of such universal geniuses as Leonardo da Vinci and Michelangelo. To convince ourselves of what a passion personal reputation and honor was to these great artists we have only to read their own personal notes, letters, and diaries. And in poetry there is no theme that is more perennial in Renaissance literature in general but in Italian literature in particular than the fame that literature can bring its creators themselves and those, too, whom it memorializes. The theme of Horace's *Exegi monumentum aere perennius* is reborn and starts a long and vigorous new life.[19]

But the very exaggeration of the Italian Renaissance pursuit of honor and glory induced its own reactions even in Italy. Even Petrarch, who is often taken as a kind of apotheosis of the Italian Renaissance spirit, has qualifications to make about the pursuit of honor in his *Secretum*, where he confesses his own pursuit of it as a sin. And in his famous *trionfi*, which started a long tradition of poetic and graphic representations of fame, the triumph of Fame is followed immediately by the triumphs of Time and Eternity, which again throws earthly fame into an almost medieval perspective with fleeting time and ageless eternity.

And in the North there was even a more persistent antipathy shown toward the pursuit of earthly glory on the part of the vast majority of writers. In practice there was probably as much vanity, pride, and worldly ambition in the North as anywhere else; but at least the theorists were, if anything, oversevere in their treatment of the whole subject of earthly glory.[20] They seemed in some way to have identified it with what they called Italianate corruption.

We have room here for only a few examples of this north-

ern Renaissance critical attitude. The following lines of Feltham
on fame are typical:

> Fame, I confess, I finde more eagerly pursued by the
> Heathen, than by Christians of these times. The Immortality
> (as they thought) of their name was to them, as the Immor-
> tality of the soul to us: A strong Reason, to persuade to
> Worthiness. Their knowledge halted in the latter; so they
> rested in the first. Which often made them sacrifice their
> lives to that, which they esteem'd above their lives, their
> Fame. Christians know a thing beyond it: And, that knowl-
> edge, causes them to give but a secondary respect to Fame;
> there being no reason, why we should neglect that, whereon
> all our future happiness depends, for that, which is nothing
> but a name, and empty air. Virtue were a kind of Misery, if
> Fame alone were all the Garland, that did crown her. Glory
> alone were a reward incompetent, for the toils of industrious
> Man. This follows him but on Earth, in Heaven is laid up a
> more Noble, more Essential recompense. Yet, because 'tis a
> fruit that springs from good actions, I must think, he that
> loves that, loveth also that which causeth it, Worthiness. In
> others; I will honour the Fame, for the deserving deeds which
> caused it. In my self, I will respect the actions, that may merit
> it.[21]

This is a view of earthly glory almost as severe as that of Saint
Augustine himself.

And Fulke Greville, in his *An Inquisition upon Fame and
Honour*, although not as critical of earthly fame as a motive of
human action as is Feltham, does ultimately denounce it. He
makes some concessions about fame acting as a unifying force
in society and states, but he ends his poem in a criticism of the
pursuit of earthly fame that is again almost Augustinian in tone.

> Who worship Fame, commit idolatry,
> Make men their god, Fortune and Time their worth.[22]

And as a final example, Thomas More might be cited. At the end of his *Utopia* he makes pride and ambition for fame the root of all the evils in society. More had seen, in the life of Cardinal Wolsey, his predecessor in the Chancellorship of England, a vivid example of the effects of pride and ambition in the life of man. It is not surprising, then, that in his own life and writings he takes a very ascetic view of the pursuit of riches and honors, and that he makes pride and ambition the root of all evils in society.

> If that one monster pride, the first and foremost of all evils, did not forbid it, the whole world would doubtless have adopted the laws of the Utopians long before this, drawn on by a rational perception of what each man's true interest is or else by the authority of Christ our Saviour, Who in His great wisdom knows what is best and in His loving kindness bids us do it. Pride measures prosperity not by her own goods but by others' wants. Pride would not deign to be a goddess, if there was no inferiors she could rule and triumph over. Her happiness shines brightly only in comparison to others' misery, and their poverty binds them and hurts them the more as her wealth is displayed. Pride is the infernal serpent that steals into the hearts of men, thwarting and holding them back from choosing the better way of life. Pride is far too deeply rooted in men's hearts to be easily torn out.[23]

The whole treatment of worldly wealth and honors in the *Utopia* suggests that, like Augustine, More identifies the pursuit of earthly honor with pride. And the Augustinian flavor in his ascetic view is not accidental, since More was a great student and admirer of Augustine. As a young man he had lectured on *The City of God* in the pulpit of his like-minded friend, John Colet, Dean of St. Paul's.

In the light of this rather persistent suspicion cast upon the pursuit of earthly glory, certain questions arose in the minds of many Christian Renaissance writers: May the Christian in any way make the pursuit of earthly fame an end in life or must he purchase heavenly glory by the constant rejection of earthly fame? The answers to these questions in the Renaissance showed the same kind of divergencies as did the earlier answers of Saint Augustine and Saint Thomas Aquinas. It remains, in the last chapters, to explore the answers to these questions in the poems of two major Renaissance poets—Spenser and Milton.

NOTES

[1] Plato, *The Republic*, translated by Francis M. Cornford (New York: Oxford University Press, 1950), pp. 306-307.

[2] *Ibid.*

[3] Saint Augustine, *The City of God*, translated by John Healey; Everyman Edition (London: J. M. Dent & Sons, Ltd., 1950), II, 58-59. All page references to *The City of God* are to this edition and will be given in the text following the citation.

[4] Saint Thomas, *Summa Theologica*, translated by Fathers of English, Dominican Province (London: Burns Oates and Washbourne, Ltd., 1935), II^a, II^{ae}, CXXIX, articulus 2, ad corpus.

[5] *Ibid*, articulus 2.

[6] *Ibid.*

[7] "Magnanimity regards two things. It regards one as its end, in so far as it is some great deed that the magnanimous man attempts in proportion to his ability. . . . The other thing that magnanimity regards is its matter, viz., honour, of which it makes right use."—*Summa*, II^a, II^{ae}, CXXXI, articulus 2, ad Iam.

[8] *Summa*, II^a, II^{ae}, CXXIX, articulus 3, ad 4.

[9] *Summa*, II^a, II^{ae}, CXXX.

[10] *Summa*, II^a, II^{ae}, CXXXI, 2 e contra.

At the very outset of his discussion of ambition Saint Thomas reiterates the principles by which a desire for honor is to be considered rational: "Honour denotes reverence shown to a person in witness of his excellence. Now two things have to be considered with regard to man's honour. The first is that a man has not from himself the thing in which he excels, for this is, as it were, something Divine in him, wherefore on this count honour is due principally, not to him but to God. The second point that calls for observation is that the thing in which man excels is given to him by God, that he may profit others thereby: wherefore a man ought so far to be pleased that others bear witness to his excellence, as this enables him to profit others" (II^a, II^{ae}, CXXXI, articulus 1, ad corpus). The principle of unselfishness in one's attitude toward honor could hardly be put more clearly than this.

11 *Ibid.*

Not every irrational desire for honor is an excess against magnanimity. Saint Thomas reminds us that it is only the irrational desire for *great* honors that is so, since magnanimity itself is the reasoned attitude that a great man takes toward great honors.

12 *Summa*, II^a, II^{ae}, CXXXII, articulus 1, ad corpus.

Saint Thomas points out in the body of this article, too, that the chief distinction between glory and honor in general is that glory implies a kind of public splendor in the recognition accorded a man's excellence that is not necessarily implied in honor.

13 That is what Saint Augustine meant when he said in the passage quoted above (page 122): ". . . so much the nearer are we to God, as we are purer from this impurity [the desire for honor]."

14 In a sense, of course, God can be said to seek glory from men since He cannot be indifferent about men's recognition of Him manifested in creation. Scripture frequently represents God as reprehending man for not acknowledging Him. But the gainer in such an acknowledgment is man and not God. Saint Thomas quotes Saint Augustine to the following effect in answer to the objection that there can be nothing wrong with seeking glory since even God Himself does so: "As Augustine says on John XIII, 13, 'you call Me Master and Lord; and you do well. (Tract. lviii in Joan): Self-complacency is fraught with danger of one who has to beware of pride. But He Who is above all, however much He may praise Himself, does not uplift Himself. For knowledge of God is our need, not His: nor does any man know Him unless he be taught of Him Who knows.' It is therefore evident that God seeks glory, not for His own sake, but for ours. In like manner a man may rightly seek his own glory for the good of others, according to Matth., V, 16, 'That they may see your good works, and glorify your Father Who is in heaven'" (II^a, II^{ae}, CXXXII, articulus 1, ad Iam).

15 II^a, II^{ae}, CXXXIII, articuli 1-2.

16 II^a, II^{ae}, CXXXI, articulus 4.

17 "But Gregory . . . did not place it [pride] among the cap-

ital vices, but held it to be the 'queen and mother of all the vices.' Hence he says: 'Pride, the queen of vices, when it has vanquished and captured the heart, forthwith delivers it into the hands of its lieutenants the seven principal vices, that they may despoil it and produce vices of all kinds," (II^a, II^{ae}, CLXII, articulus 8, ad corpus).

[18] Geoffrey Chaucer, *The House of Fame*, III, ll. 1615-1656.

[19] See Edwin B. Benjamin, "Fame, Poetry, and the Order of History in the Literature of the English Renaissance," *Studies in the Renaissance*, VI (1959), 64-84.

[20] Miss Isabel E. Rathborne has the following observation to make in this connection: "Writing in the Florence of Lorenzo de' Medici, Poliziano exhibits that serene paganism which characterizes the Italian Renaissance at its height. To him, as to the ancients, the thirst for glory could not but seem the noblest of all human desires. But for the Italians of the previous century, over which the shadow of the Christian Middle Ages still brooded, as for the later poets of the northern nations in whom the spirit of the Renaissance was modified by the sterner doctrines of the Reformation, the golden trumpet of fame sounded less clearly. They were troubled by doubts. Was not this Fame after all a pagan goddess, sister to Fortune, as Chaucer indeed pictures her, bestowing her favors indifferently upon the just and the unjust? Were not the lamentable falls of famous princes and mighty empires a warning that earthly glory is rooted in the sin of pride, and doomed to a swift decay? Even if we distinguish between ill-gotten power or the mere reputation which may be acquired by fraud and the true honor which is the reward of virtue, what is mortal righteousness in the sight of God? Are we not all sinners, doomed to die for our sins? Is not this earth, covered with the ruins of temples and palaces built by the ancients, who were so much wiser than we, itself a vast *memento mori*? And should not these ruins remind us that the earth itself and its fair vault of heaven shall themselves disappear before God makes all things new? To trust in earthly glory, to seek fame as the earnest of immortality, is not this to set up the Earthly City against the City of God?"—Reprinted from *The Meaning of Spenser's Fairyland*, by Isabel Rathborne, Columbia University Press, 1937.

[21] Owen Feltham, *Resolves: Divine, Moral, Political* (London: Printed for A. Seile, 1670), p. 25.

22 Fulke Greville, *Works,* edited by Alexander B. Grosart (London: Blackburn, 1870), II, 73.

23 Thomas More, *Utopia,* translated by H. V. S. Ogden (New York: Appleton-Century-Crofts, Inc., 1949), pp. 81-82.

CHAPTER EIGHT

Magnanimity in Spenser

*"With which he [the good Courtier] kindleth his
    ambitious sprights
To like desire and praise of noble fame,
The onely upshot whereto he doth ayme:
For all his mind on honour fixed is
To which he levels all his purposis.
And in his Princes service spends his dayes,
Not so much for to gaine, or for to raise
Himselfe to high degree, as for his grace,
And in his liking to winne worthy place."*
    EDMUND SPENSER: *Mother Hubberds Tale*, ll. 768-776

> *"Yet is* Cleopolis *for earthly frame,
>   The fairest peece, that eye beholden can:
>   And well beseemes all knights of noble name,
>   That covet in th'immortal booke of fame,
>   To be eternized, that same to haunt,
>   And doen their service to that sovereigne Dame,
>   That glorie does to them for guerdon graunt;
> For she is heavenly borne, and heaven may iustly
>   vaunt."*
>   EDMUND SPENSER: *The Faerie Queene*, I, x, 59

Among the Renaissance writers north of the Alps who treated
the subject of the pursuit of honor, Spenser had an almost
unique position. The vast majority of these northern writers,
especially in England, took a somewhat critical and suspicious

view of the whole subject of earthly fame and glory and thus continued and emulated some of the views of Saint Augustine on the subject. But Spenser from the first was more tolerant of the pursuit of earthly honor and glory. In this area, as in many others, recent scholarship is more frequently recognizing that he expressed views that relate him to Thomas Aquinas rather than to either Aristotle or Saint Augustine; however, eclectic that he was, he did draw many ideas from both these philosophers.[1]

We get our first glimpse of Spenser's attitude toward the subject of earthly glory in his rather unsuccessful beast fable, *Mother Hubberds Tale*.[2] The theme of that whole poem is the ambitioning of place, position, and worldly honor and glory. Ambition, we recall, for both Aristotle and Saint Thomas, is an excess against that nameless virtue which should guide the mediocre person in his pursuit of honor. When a mediocre person seeks a place, position, and consequent honors which are higher than his merits warrant, he is ambitious. Saint Thomas, of course, unlike Aristotle, admitted that even the magnanimous man is capable of such excess. But unquestionably the vice of the Ape and the Fox in Spenser's fable is the excess of mediocre characters.

It is not so much the fact that Spenser makes ambition the theme of his fable that interests us here but rather the tone in which he handles his subject. *Mother Hubberds Tale* is no Augustinian excoriation of all earthly glory; nor a poem on the medieval theme, *vanitas vanitatum*. On the contrary, in the portrait of

> . . . the brave Courtier, in whose beauteous thought
> Regard of honour harbours more than ought
> —*M.H.T.*, ll. 717-718.[3]

we are given to understand that there is nothing wrong with the pursuit of honor if it is based upon virtue and service and not upon mere pretense. As a matter of fact, it is with the utmost approval that Spenser records that the good Courtier fills his memory with the accounts

> Of Natures workes, of heavens continuall course,
> Of forreine lands, of people different,
> Of kingdomes change, of divers government,
> Of dreadfull battailes of renowned Knights;
> With which he kindleth his ambitious sprights
> To like desire and praise of noble fame,
> The onely upshot whereto he doth ayme:
> For all his minde on honour fixed is,
> To which he levels all his purposis. . . .
>
> —*M.H.T.*, ll. 764-772.

But in the very next lines of the poem, Spenser also makes it clear that the basis of the honor on which his "brave Courtier" has his mind fixed is an unself-centered service of his Prince.

> And in his Princes service spends his dayes,
> Not so much for to gaine, or for to raise
> Himselfe to high degree, as for his grace,
> And in his liking to winne worthie place;
> Through due deserts and comely carriage,
> In whatso please employ his personage,
> That may be matter meete to gaine him praise;
> For he is fit to use in all assayes,
> Whether for Armes and warlike amenaunce,
> Or else for wise and civill governaunce.
> For he is practiz'd well in policie,
> And thereto doth his Courting most applie:
> To learne the enterdeale of Princes strange,
> To marke th'intent of Counsells, and the change
> Of states, and eke of private men somewhile,
> Supplanted by fine falshood and faire guile;
> Of all the which he gathereth, what is fit
> T'enrich the storehouse of his powerfull wit,

> Which through wise speaches, and grave conference
> He daylie eekes, and brings to excellence.
> Such is the rightfull Courtier in his kinde.
> —*M.H.T.*, ll. 773-793.

In this first draft of Spenser's magnanimous man, we discover a large element of the Roman concept of civic duty, but colored by the Elizabethan political world view in which a great man at court could perhaps do his country as great a service in the council chamber as on the battlefield.

It is in the light of this picture of the ideal Courtier's rightful regard for honor that the wrongful scramble for position and honor by the two "base losels" of Spenser's fable must be read. The Ape and the Foxe, by their own admission, have neither the accomplishments nor virtues which would win them place, position, and honor; but this does not prevent them from ambitioning to attain the very highest positions of state and the honors that go with them:

> The Foxe and th'Ape disliking of their evill
> And hard estate, determined to seeke
> Their fortunes farre abroad.
> —*M.H.T.*, ll. 46-48.

And by making a fox and an ape the characters in his fable of ambition, Spenser is saying that, in the absence of the virtues and self-sacrificing service that should win one position and honor, the imitativeness of the ape and the craftiness of the fox may be able to purchase or steal what genuine virtue and unself-centered accomplishments would merit.

What is wrong with the Ape's and the Foxe's ambition, Spenser makes clear, is not their pursuit of honor, but their pursuit of greater honor than they deserve, and their pursuit of it in such a way as to defy both God and their neighbor.

> What else then did he [the Ape] by progression,
> But mocke high God himselfe, whom they [Divines]
> professe?

[140]

But what car'd he for God, or godlinesse?
All his care was himselfe how to advaunce.
                                    —*M.H.T.*, ll. 842-845.

Saint Thomas had said that the pursuit of honor by any man,
even the magnanimous man, can be excessive if it ignores one's
dependence upon God for the position and honor one has received and also if it ignores the fact that such position, power,
and honors are given as a trust for one's neighbor. In this key
passage of the poem Spenser presents his climbers as offending
on both counts.

In contrast to the rightful Courtier's unselfish service of his
Prince, all the care of these "losels" is to advance themselves.
Their blatant selfishness is evident on every step of their climb
upward: as shepherds, they despoil the yeomen's flock; as
clerics, they ignore the demands of their parishioners; as cour-
tiers, they are intent only on their own advancement and cor-
rupt everybody with whom they come in contact; and finally,
in the usurped position of kingship, when no further advancement is possible,

Then gan he [the Ape] rule and tyrannize at will,
Like as the Foxe did guide his graceless skill,
And all wylde beasts made vassals of his pleasures,
And with their spoyles enlarg'd his private treasures.
No care of justice, nor no rule of reason,
No temperance, nor no regard of season
Did thenceforth ever enter in his minde,
But crueltie, the signe of currish kinde,
And sdeignfull pride, and wilfull arrogaunce;
Such followes those whom fortune doth advaunce.
                                    —*M.H.T.*, ll. 1127-1136.

The result of all this false ambition, of course, is utter chaos
in the body politic; so much so that Jove himself is at last moved
to send Mercury down to arouse the sleeping king to eject the
ambitious usurpers and restore order in the kingdom. And there

[141]

is more than a suggestion that the king himself is at fault for having slept so soundly that he made it possible for these "javels" to have usurped the august prerogatives of kingship in the first place.

This is Spenser's first indictment of a false ambitioning of honor, but the whole import of *Mother Hubberds Tale* is that there is nothing nobler for the "right gentle and brave Courtier," than the "regard of honour" upon which all his mind is fixed. So far is Spenser from discounting the pursuit of earthly glory that he makes it the point to which his truly great man at court "levels all his purposis."

When Spenser came to write his major work, *The Faerie Queene*, his ideas about earthly glory did not change. As a matter of fact, the whole theme of *Mother Hubberds Tale* is repeated in the Philotime episode of Book II. Book II tells the story of the adventures of Sir Guyon, who, in the moral allegory, represents temperance, and, if Professor Woodhouse[4] is correct, the natural virtue of temperance, or man guided by reason rather than by the supernatural action of grace—the power that is operating in the vicissitudes of the Redcrosse Knight in Book I.

In canto 7 Sir Guyon undergoes a series of temptations at the hands of Mammon. Mammon tempts him to riches in various guises, but, unlike the Redcrosse Knight, who finds the virtuous life a Stoic battle and sometimes a losing one, Sir Guyon, with a great deal of Aristotelian self-assurance, brushes all Mammon's temptations aside as ridiculously unreasonable. As a last resort, Mammon tempts him to succumb to the honor that only riches can give. It is a temptation to what Aristotle had called φιλοτιμία or excessive love of honor or ambition. The temptation is presented in the guise of a fair lady, Philotime, and everything about the lady herself and her surroundings and companions reveals Spenser's evalution of the vice of ambition. Like the Ape and the Foxe in *Mother Hubberds Tale*, Philotime is a counterfeit:

Her face right wondrous faire did seeme to bee,
That her broad beauties beam great brightnes threw
Through the dim shade, that all men might it see:
Yet was not that same her owne native hew,
But wrought by art and counterfetted shew.

—*F.Q.*, II, vii, 45.

And the rout that swarms about her throne, trying to catch hold of her glistening chain that stretched from hell to heaven, also resembles the virtueless scramble for place and honor of the Ape and the Foxe.

There, as in glistring glory she did sit,
　She held a great gold chaine ylincked well,
　Whose upper end to highest heaven was knit,
　And lower part did reach to lowest Hell;
　And all that preace did round about her swell,
　To catchen hold of that long chaine, thereby
　To clime aloft, and others to excell:
　That was *Ambition*, rash desire to sty,
And every lincke thereof a step of dignity.

Some thought to raise themselves to high degree,
　By riches and unrighteous reward,
　Some by close shouldring, some by flatteree;
　Others through friends, others for base regard;
　And all by wrong wayes for themselves prepard.
　Those that were up themselves, kept others low,
　Those that were low themselves, held others hard,
　Ne suffred them to rise or greater grow,
But every one did strive his fellow downe to throw.

—*F.Q.*, II, vii, 46-47.

Sir Guyon, who represents the quintessence of natural temperance, is no more moved by this spectacle of false honor, Mammon's daughter, than he was by the false blandishments of his riches. He is so sure of himself, in fact, that he indulges in a little irony in his response to Mammon's offer of his daughter Philotime's hand in marriage.

[143]

Gramercy *Mammon* (said the gentle knight)
  For so great grace and offred high estate;
  But I, that am fraile flesh and earthly wight,
  Unworthy match for such immortall mate
  My selfe well wote, and mine unequall fate;
  And were I not, yet is my trouth yplight,
  And love avowd to other Lady late,
  That to remove the same I have no might.
              —*F.Q.*, II, vii, 50.

Sir Guyon, like the brave Courtier in *Mother Hubberds Tale*, contemns Philotime, false honor, not because he despises honor but because he is vowed to the service of his queen Gloriana, or true honor.

In *Mother Hubberds Tale* and in the Philotime episode of *The Faerie Queene*, Spenser is chiefly concerned with revealing the nature of false honor or ambition, but in *The Faerie Queene* in general he is very positively concerned with the true basis of honor and glory. In fact, it is glory and the virtues of magnanimity and magnificence, which gauge the national pursuit of it, that are the central theme of the whole poem. Spenser himself tells us as much in his famous Letter to Sir Walter Raleigh. He represents Arthur, he tells Sir Walter, as having

> . . . seene in a dream or vision the Faery Queen, with whose excellent beauty ravished, he awaking resolved to seeke her out, and so being by Merlin armed, and by Timon throughly instructed, he went to seeke her forth in Faery land. In that Faery Queene I meane glory in my general intention, but in particular I conceive the most excellent and glorious person of our souveraine the Queene, and her kingdome in Faery land.[5]

What Arthur is in quest of, then, in the poem is glory—but glory based on service to the Queen. In the large historical context of the poem as planned, Arthur would probably have found and wed the Queen, thus strengthening the honor of the Tudor dynasty by associating it with ancient Welsh roots as Virgil had associated Rome with the ancient roots of Troy; but in the moral allegory, the chief point of Arthur's quest of Gloriana is made without this final marriage. For spenser goes on to say that

> . . . in the person of Prince Arthure I sette forth magnificence in particular, which vertue for that (according to Aristotle and the rest) it is the perfection of all the rest, and conteineth in it them all.[6]

In Spenser's plan, then, Arthur represents magnificence. Recent scholars, such as Professor Maloney,[7] have pointed out that, in Saint Thomas and other commentators on Aristotle, magnificence merely means the external impressive manifestation in deeds (*magna facta*) of the internal virtue of magnanimity (*magna anima*). Since Arthur represents magnificence, that virtue rooted in magnanimity, which is the virtue primarily concerned with the rational attitude toward honor, it is in the person and actions of Arthur in the poem that Spenser chiefly intends to give his archetypal image of the true and rational pursuit of honor and glory. And on every level of allegory in the poem, Arthur merits glory through service: to Gloriana herself in the political and ecclesiastical allegories,[8] and, in the moral allegory, to the knight who needs his help at a critical moment of his career. Besides this, Arthur, as an allegorization of magnificence (which includes magnanimity), embodies in himself all the virtues and is thus the pre-eminently shining example of the virtue being allegorized in each individual book. And he becomes, in each book, as Spenser himself puts it, a "profitable and gratious ensample" of the basis of true glory as it is rooted in the practice of virtue and the service of others.

But it is not merely in the person of Arthur that the theme of the quest for glory operates in *The Faerie Queene*. Each of the knights in the separate books is also in the service of Gloriana; and since they represent separate virtues, all of which are contained in the virtue of magnificence, they are, in a sense, all contained in Arthur's pursuit of glory. But that glory is a powerful motivation of each of them is also made explicit at every turn in the poem. And, as in the case of Arthur himself, this motivation is frequently combined with the motive of love

> For love does alwayes bring forth bounteous deeds,
> And in each gentle hart desire of honour breeds.
> —*F.Q.*, III, i, 49.

Though it is true that the motif of glory plays an important role in every book of *The Faerie Queene*, it is given a particularly full treatment in the story of the Redcrosse Knight. We would rather expect this to be the case, since, in Book I, Spenser is giving us his complete view of man's earthly condition—supernatural as well as natural. In this enlarged perspective he can ask and answer the question which plagued so many Renaissance writers: Has a Christian any right to pursue earthly glory or must he be content with the pursuit of heavenly Glory? The story of the Redcrosse Knight is, among other things, an answer to that question.

There is no doubt whatever about the motive of the Redcrosse Knight. He also serves Gloriana and is off on a venture of her giving. He accepts her commission precisely to win her praise and establish his own reputation:

> Upon a great adventure he was bond,
>   That greatest *Gloriana* to him gave,
>   That greatest Glorious Queene of *Faerie* lond,
>   To winne him worship, and her grace to have,
>   Which of all earthly things he most did crave;
>   And ever as he rode, his hart did earne
>   To prove his puissance in battell brave
>   Upon his foe, and his new force to learne;
> Upon his foe, a Dragon horrible and stearne.
> —*F.Q.*, I, i, 3.[9]

Armed with both the natural and supernatural virtues, and accompanied by the Dwarfe, natural temperance, and Una, supernatural wisdom, he is eager to prove his mettle in battle. But completely inexperienced, he has a lot to learn; and he learns it the hard way. Unlike the secure Sir Guyon, who is subjected to temptations which he rejects with the utmost confidence in order to demonstrate what temperance is, the Redcrosse Knight is subjected to a whole series of temptations to which he succumbs in order to learn humility through humiliation.

Saint Thomas and many other Christian commentators on Aristotle had insisted that the Christian's pursuit of honor must be limited by both humility and charity. Spenser is at pains to underline both these conditions in the exploits of the Redcrosse Knight, his Christian Everyman. He represents, Spenser reminds us, Christian holiness, but not, like Sir Guyon, a perfected virtue but rather holiness in the making.

In the rash hardihood of his young, untested powers, what the Redcrosse Knight most needs to learn is his dependence upon God for achieving anything which will merit the honor he seeks. It takes him the whole of the action of the first ten cantos of Book I to learn it, and he learns it only after he has sunk into the depths of the degradation of Orgoglio's dungeon.

The steps by which Spenser represents the progressive degradation of the Redcrosse Knight[10] are particularly pertinent to the subject of humility as a limitation on the Christian pursuit of personal fame and glory, because they climax in a sin of pride. In each of the downward steps, the Redcrosse Knight rejects the vice to which he is tempted when he sees it clearly for what it is, only to succumb to it almost immediately when it approaches him in disguise. In the Cave of Error he is, as a matter of fact, overquick to attack the hideous monster and has to be cautioned against rashness by both Una and the Dwarfe. But seeing Monstrous Error clearly in all its grossness, he does manage to kill it, only to be caught in its snares when it attacks him in the hypocritical deceptions of Archimago. The same is true of sensuality. He is revolted by what he considers the sensuality of Una at the cottage of Archimago, but he himself shortly thereafter falls prey to the deceitful charms of Duessa. And finally, and most relevant to our theme here, he has no difficulty recognizing the aberrations of pride when they are openly paraded before him in the masque at the House of Pride, but, further corrupted and deceived by Duessa, he almost immediately falls into the grips of Orgoglio, the worst kind of spiritual pride or excessive self-confidence. Separated from both Una and the Dwarfe, from the guidance of both reason and revealed truth, he is a victim of his own self-reliance, and ends a helpless prisoner in the dark dungeon of Orgoglio. It is only when he has fallen thus low, and is utterly unable to help himself, that he realizes how dependent upon God's grace he really is. It is at this juncture that God's grace comes to him in the person of Arthur; that he is freed from the consequences of his own exaggerated self-reliance; that Orgoglio is overcome by Arthur; that Duessa is exposed for what she is; and that the humbled Redcrosse Knight starts again on his long upward road to holiness and an understanding of the conditions necessary for winning true earthly glory.

But it is important for the understanding of Spenser's complete attitude toward the pursuit of earthly glory to note that, as Professor Rathborne has well pointed out,[11] he does not, like St. Augustine, identify pride and earthly glory. In fact, he makes it quite clear in the House of Pride that Lucifera is a counterfeit Gloriana. She is as false as Lady Philotime of Book II and as the Ape and the Foxe in *Mother Hubberds Tale*. Everything about her house, her person, and her surroundings is false. Her castle looks strong and beautiful, but it is constructed of loose brick without mortar and is built on shifting sand. It makes a brave show of gilded towers in the front but is crumbling to pieces in the rear, and the decay is only thinly disguised by a coat of paint. And the lady herself, in her dress, her bearing, and her actions, "doth protest too much." It is all overdone. The "endless richesse" and "sumptuous shew," the "glistring gold and peerless precious stone," "cloth of state," "royal robes and gorgeous array" do not quite add up, in the content, to queenliness. She studies her countenance in a mirror and imagines herself dimming the sun itself, but in a neat simile Spenser exposes her real affinity to the sun.

> Exceeding shone, like *Phoebus* fairest childe,
> That did presume his fathers firie wayne,
> And flaming mouthes of steedes unwonted wilde
> Through highest heaven with weaker hand to rayne;
> Proud of such glory and advancement vaine,
> While flashing beames do daze his feeble eyen,
> He leaves the welkin way most beaten plaine,
> And rapt with whirling wheeles, inflames the skyen,
> With fire not made to burne, but fairely for to shyne.
>
> So proud she shyned in her Princely state,
> Looking to heaven; for earth she did disdayne,
> And sitting high; for lowly she did hate.
> —*F.Q.*, I, iv, 9-10.

Everything about her is false. Pride cannot face the truth about its origins.

> Of griesly *Pluto* she the daughter was,
> And sad *Proserpina* the Queene of hell;
> Yet did she thinke her pearelesse worth to pas
> That parentage, with pride so did she swell,
> And thundring *Iove*, that high in heaven doth dwell,
> And wield the world, she claymed for her syre,
> Or if that any else did *Iove* excell:
> For to the highest she did still aspyre,
> Or if ought higher were then that, did it desyre.
> —*F.Q.*, I, iv, 11.

Like everything else, both her name and her throne she holds on false pretenses.

> And proud *Lucifera* men did her call,
> That made her selfe a Queene, and crownd to be,

Yet rightfull kingdome she had none at all,
Ne heritage of native soveraintie,
But did usurpe with wrong and tyrannie
Upon the scepter, which she now did hold:
Ne ruld her Realmes with lawes, but pollicie,
And strong advizement of six wisards old,
That with their counsels bad her kingdome did uphold.
—*F.Q.* I, iv, 12.

Lucifera, the false light-bearer and daughter of the father of lies, is a rescript of the usurpers in *Mother Hubberds Tale*. The consequence of all her deceit and pretense, of course, is chaos, injustice, and tyranny. The Redcrosse Knight sees all this, and has a vivid reminder of the consequences of the reign of Pride in the "loathsome lazars" that lay along the castle's hedges. And his trusty Dwarfe also tells him about the victims of pride who have tumbled from exalted places of state and pine now in dungeons underneath Pride's castle. The Dwarfe's narrative amounts to a veritable *casus virorum illustrium* including exalted men from the king of Babylon to Pompey and Antonius and women from Semiramnis to Cleopatra.

Besides the endlesse routs of wretched thralles,
Which thither were assembled day by day,
From all the world after their wofull falles,
Through wicked pride, and wasted wealthes decay.
But most of all, which in that Dongeon lay
Fell from high Princes courts, or Ladies bowres,
Where they in idle pompe, or wanton play,
Consumed had their goods, and thriftlesse howres,
And lastly throwne themselves into these heavy stowres.
—*F.Q.*, I, v, 51.

With this reminder of the fall of Princes "which all through that great Princesse pride did fall," the Redcrosse Knight leaves her castle in disgust, and his mood is not improved as

A donghill of dead carkases he spide;
The dreadful spectacle of that sad house of *Pride*.
—*F.Q.*, I, v, 53.

But the sight is not dreadful enough to save him from being allured by Duessa into the power of an even more disgust-
ing impersonation of pride, the puffed-up giant Orgoglio. When
Arthur rescues him from pride's dungeon he himself is an
emaciated skeleton of his former self—

Whose feeble thighes, unhable to uphold
His pined corse, him scarse to light could beare,
A ruefull spectacle of death and ghastly drere.

His sad dull eyes deepe sunck in hollow pits,
Could not endure th'unwonted sunne to view;
His bare thin cheekes for want of better bits,
And empty sides deceived of their dew,
Could make a stony hart his hap to rew;
His rawbone armes, whose mighty brawned bowrs
Were wont to rive steele plates, and helmets hew,
Were cleane consum'd, and all his vitall powres
Decayd, and all his flesh shronk up like withered flowres.
—*F.Q.*, I, viii, 40-41.

What a graphic picture of the helplessness of proud, self-reliant
man without the grace of God. Thus painfully has the Redcrosse Knight learned that he can do nothing of note in the
Kingdom of God without His grace. So weak is he and so
vividly is he impressed with his own weakness that he almost
succumbs to despair. But to deepen and broaden the lesson of
humility and to strengthen him with hope, Una brings him to
the House of Holiness.

There he is in a different world. And Spenser goes to great
pains to make the House of Holiness as obviously different from
the House of Pride as possible. In the Castle of Lucifera, everything was ostentation and pretense; in the House of Dame

[151]

Caelia, everything is the soul of simplicity and sincerity. While Lucifera decks herself in Persian splendor, seats herself on an exalted throne, and affects the manners of an empress, Dame Caelia appears as a simple matron and mother of a family, fingering her beads. In contrast to the flattery, envy, and backbiting that reign at Lucifera's court, a disarming guilelessness and charity pervade the household of Dame Caelia. Malvenu and Vanity are the porter and usher at the court of Lucifera, while Humiltá, Reverence, and Obedience serve Dame Caelia. Lucifera herself is a sterile maid, and her court is fruitful only of the capital sins; in contrast, Dame Caelia is the happy mother of three daughters, Fidelia, Speranza, and Charissa; and Charissa herself is the mother of a brood of happy children. Humiltá and Charissa, humility and charity, are the virtues which pervade the atmosphere of the House of Holiness.

It is in this atmosphere that the Redcrosse Knight is put to school, at first to Fidelia and Speranza, to deepen his supernatural knowledge of himself in relationship to God and to strengthen his hope. In the House of Holiness he gradually is taken through the three ways of the spiritual life, the purgative, the illuminative, and the unitative.[12] The experience is costly to self, but unlike the sterility of the House of Pride, it fructifies in good works. It is Charissa, Christian Charity, who conducts the Redcrosse Knight to the Hospital of Mercie and there instructs him in the seven works of mercy:

> There she awhile him stayes, him selfe to rest,
>   That to the rest more able he might bee:
>   During which time, in every good behest
>   And godly worke of Almes and charitee
>   She him instructed with great industree;
>   Shortly therein so perfect he became,
>   That from the first unto the last degree,
>   His mortall life he learned had to frame
> In holy righteousness, without rebuke or blame.
>   —*F.Q.*, I, x, 45.

It is only when he has thus been perfected in humility and charity that he is at last led by Charissa up the Mount of Contemplation and turned over to the venerable hermit Contemplation himself, who will give him his final instruction in the true relationship between earthly and heavenly glory. Along with other things, his experience in the two opposed houses of Lucifera and Dame Caelia has already taught him that pride is the service of self at the expense of others, and that Christian holiness is the service of God and of one's neighbors at the expense of self. He will be reminded of that once more by the Hermit on the Mount of Contemplation.

As they stand on that mount, the Redcrosse Knight is given a glimpse of the glory of the Heavenly Jerusalem—a City

> Whose wals and towres were builded high and strong
> Of perle and precious stone, that earthly tong
> Cannot describe, nor wit of man can tell;
> Too high a ditty for my simple song;
> The City of the great king hight it well,
> Wherein eternall peace and happinesse doth dwell.
>
> As he thereon stod gazing, he might see
>   The blessed Angels to and fro descend
>   From highest heaven, in gladsome compance,
>   And with great joy into that Citie wend,
>   As commonly as frend does with his frend.
>   —*F.Q.*, I, x, 55-56.

Redcrosse is properly awed by his first glimpse of the glory of this Heavenly City, and immediately compares it with the earthly glory of the fairest city he had seen till then—the great Cleopolis.

> Till now, said then the knight, I weened well,
>   That great *Cleopolis*, where I have beene,
>   In which that fairest *Faerie Queene* doth dwell,
>   The fairest Citie was, that might be seene;

[153]

And that bright towre all built of christall cleene,
Panthea, seemd the brightest thing, that was:
But now by proofe all otherwise I weene;
For this great Citie that does far surpas,
And this bright Angels towre quite dims that towre of glas.
                                                    —*F.Q.*, I, x, 58.

The comment of the Old Hermit on this exclamation of the Redcrosse Knight is the best indication of the difference between Spenser's attitude toward the relationship between the glory of the earthly City and that of the Heavenly City and the attitude of Saint Augustine:

Most trew, then said the holy aged man;
    Yet is *Cleopolis* for earthly frame,
    The fairest peece, that eye beholden can:
    And well beseemes all knights of noble name,
    That covet in th'immortall booke of fame
    To be eternized, that same to haunt,
    And doen their service to that soveraigne Dame,
    That glorie does to them for guerdon graunt:
For she is heavenly borne, and heaven may justly vaunt.
                                                    —*F.Q.*, I, x, 59.

So far is Spenser from identifying earthly glory with pride, as Saint Augustine had done, that he here makes Gloriana a queen of heavenly birth and makes service to her the highest and most worthy achievement of a noble knight. The Redcrosse Knight himself is congratulated by the Hermit for his dedication to and service of "her grace."

Then, like Anchises in the underworld pointing out to Aeneas the glory of the Rome-to-be, the Hermit gives the Redcrosse Knight a prevision of himself as Saint George in the eternal glory and peace of the Heavenly Jerusalem. Like the Apostles on Mount Tabor, this vision so enraptures Redcrosse that he wants to take up his abode in the Heavenly Jerusalem immediately:

O let me not (quoth he) then turne againe
    Backe to the world, whose joyes so fruitlesse are;
    But let me here for aye in peace remaine,
    Or streight way on that last long voyage fare,
    That nothing may my present hope empare.
                    —*F.Q.*, I, x, 63.

But the Hermit's answer makes clear again that Spenser conceived the pursuit of glory in the active life in time a means of meriting the peace and glory of the Heavenly Jerusalem in eternity:

That may not be (said he) ne maist thou yit
    Forgo that royall maides bequeathed care,
    Who did her cause into thy hand commit,
Till from her cursed foe thou have her freely quit.
                    —*F.Q.*, I, x, 63.

The hermit does grant, however, that the Redcrosse Knight may eventually think of abandoning earthly conquest in favor of the Heavenly Jerusalem, but this is only *after* he has won his victory in Gloriana's Cleopolis.

But when thou famous victorie hast wonne,
    And high emongst all knights hast hong thy shield,
    Thenceforth the suit of earthly conquest shonne,
    And wash thy hands from guilt of bloudy field:
For bloud can nought but sin, and wars but sorrowes yield.

Then seeke this path, that I to thee presage,
    Which after all to heaven shall thee send;
    Then peaceably thy painefull pilgrimage
    To yonder same *Hierusalem* do bend,
    Where is for thee ordaind a blessed end:
    For thou emongst those Saints, whom thou doest see,
    Shalt be a Saint, and thine owne nations frend
    And Patrone: thou Saint *George* shalt called bee,
    Saint *George* of mery England, the signe of victoree.
                    —*F.Q.*, I, x, 60-61.

This was to be his eventual destiny; but he would win it by an earthly victory over Una's dragon. As a matter of fact, he does leave the Mount of Contemplation and slay the dragon, and the last we hear of him is that he is on his way back to the court of Gloriana to report his victory and claim his mede of earthly honor for the deed.

This is Spenser's answer to the question: May a Christian engage in the pursuit of earthly glory? Unlike Saint Augustine, he does not identify earthly glory with pride, and so does not condemn the pursuit of it as pagan and unworthy of a Christian. But the whole adventure of the Redcrosse Knight should also make abundantly clear that Spenser puts upon the pursuit of earthly glory the same limitations of humility and charity as did Saint Thomas Aquinas and many other like-minded commentators on Aristotle. The place of Humiltá and Charissa in the House of Holiness only underline what the action of the whole book dramatizes. If there were any doubt about the necessity of humility for the Christian knight's pursuit of honor as Spenser conceives it, the following almost Pauline statement, which might serve as a text for the whole of Book I, would put it beyond the pale of doubt:

> Ne let the man ascribe it to his skill,
> That thorough grace hath gained victory.
> If any strength we have, it is to ill,
> But all the good is Gods, both power and eke will.
> —*F.Q.*, I, x, 1.

It is this willingness to concede respectability to the pursuit of earthly honor and glory by a Christian as long as it is limited by due humility and charity that makes Spenser's treatment of the subject fairly unique[13] among northern writers. In general they tended to look upon the quest of Lady Fame as somehow a part of Italianate corruption.

NOTES

[1] In an unpublished dissertation at the University of Chicago (1941), Miss Viola Blackburn Hulbert has demonstrated rather convincingly that it was commentators in the tradition of Thomas Aquinas rather than Aristotle himself on whom Spenser relied for his discussion of the virtues. See her dissertation, "Spenser's Twelve Moral Virtues 'According to Aristotle and the Rest.'"

[2] In an unpublished master's thesis (1950) which I directed at Saint Louis University, Miss Mary Elizabeth O'Connor has made a study of the reason for the relative failure of *Mother Hubberds Tale* as a beast fable. In the course of the thesis she relates the theme of the poem to the whole question of Aristotelian and Thomistic magnanimity. See her thesis, "A Study of the Failure of Spenser's *Mother Hubberds Tale* as a Beast Fable," pp. 82-93.

[3] Edmund Spenser, "Mother Hubberds Tale," *The Poetical Works*, edited by J. C. Smith and E. De Selincourt (London: Oxford University Press, 1935). All quotations from Spenser are from this edition. Hereafter reference will be made to lines of the poems *Mother Hubberds Tale* (*M.H.T.*) and *The Faerie Queene* (*F.Q.*) after the quotations in the text.

[4] A. S. P. Woodhouse, "Nature and Grace in *The Faerie Queene*," *English Literary History*, XVI (1949), 194-228.

[5] Spenser, "The Letter to Sir Walter Raleigh," *The Poetical Works of Edmund Spenser*, p. 407.

[6] *Ibid.*

[7] Michael F. Maloney, "Saint Thomas and Spenser's Virtue of Magnificence," *Journal of English and Germanic Philology*, LII (1953), 58-62.

[8] See Edwin A. Greenlaw, *Studies in Spenser's Historical Allegory* (Baltimore: The Johns Hopkins Press, 1932). This is still the best treatment of the historical allegory in *The Faerie Queene*. Miss Rathborne has pointed out that a fairly unique feature of Spenser's treatment of Arthur's pursuit of glory is the identification of this pursuit with the cult of love: "By making Glory herself the object of his hero's love, Spenser was able to combine in his central story of Arthur's quest for Gloriana two popular Renaissance themes, the desire for earthly immortality through fame, and the cult of love as a stimulus for noble action."—*The Meaning of*

Spenser's Fairyland (New York: Columbia University Press, 1937), p. 17.

Miss Rathborne's excellent discussion of Spenser's whole treatment of the theme of glory in *The Faerie Queene* deserves more attention than it has received in Spenser circles. It throws light on the very heart of the poem as Spenser conceived it.

[9] Again, when the Redcrosse Knight is awaiting the morning on which he will fight the pagan knight, Sansfoy, Spenser remarks:

> The noble hart, that harbours vertuous thought,
> And is with child of glorious great intent,
> Can never rest, untill it forth have brought
> Th' eternall brood of glorie excellent:
> Such restlesse passion did all night torment
> The flaming corage of that Faery knight,
> Devizing, how that doughtie turnament
> With greatest honour he achieven might;
> Still did he wake, and still did watch for dawning light.
>   —*F.Q.*, I, i.

[10] See Kerby Neill, "The Degradation of the Red Cross Knight," *English Literary History, XIX* (1952), 173-190.

[11] "In the two antitypes of Gloriana, Acrasia and Philotime, Spenser expresses a view of the relations between pleasure, ambition, and earthly glory which is quite in accord with Augustine. But where Augustine makes earthly glory synonymous with pride, Spenser separates the two conceptions, presenting them in the two sharply contrasted figures of Gloriana and Lucifera."—Rathborne, *op. cit.*, p. 12.

[12] Joseph B. Collins, *Christian Mysticism in the Elizabethan Age with Its Background in Mystical Methodology* (Baltimore: The Johns Hopkins Press, 1940). See "The House of Holiness," pp. 192-203, in which Spenser's use of the three ways of the spiritual life in the House of Holiness is discussed.

[13] Edwin B. Benjamin in his essay, "Fame, Poetry, and History," already referred to in the previous chapter, points out that Spenser and Michael Drayton are rather of one mind in expressing this more positive view of the place of fame and glory in a good man's life. He sums up the point of view thus: "The tradition of tragedy is fairly dark and gloomy, with Fame acting as an agent of justice; a more positive use is the glorification of Fame as a

stimulus to achievement. She works upon both the man of action and the man of letters, stirring them to noble deeds that will win for them immortality and at the same time inspire future generations. In this connection a desire for Fame is essentially good: Fame is not separated from Truth or Virtue, nor does earthly Fame necessarily compete with heavenly immortality. In the hierarchy of moral values Fame is never elevated to the status of Truth, Virtue, or Salvation, but as a means to them and a by-product of them she has a dignified place of her own. There is something rather Platonic about Fame in this aspect, as she leads and directs man's spirit upwards."—*Op. cit.*, p. 72. This statement applies particularly well to the attitude of Spenser revealed in the Mount of Contemplation episode in Book I of *The Faerie Queene*.

CHAPTER NINE

Magnanimity in Milton

"Since first this Subject for Heroic Song
Pleas'd me long choosing, and beginning late;
Not sedulous by Nature to indite
Warrs, hitherto the onely Argument
Heroic deem'd, Chief Maisterie to dissect
With long and tedious havoc fabl'd Knights
In Battels feign'd; the better fortitude
Of Patience, and Heroic Martyrdom
Unsung."
JOHN MILTON: Paradise Lost, IX, ll. 25-33

"But if there be in glory aught of good,
It may by means far different be attain'd
Without ambition, war, or violence;
By deeds of peace, by wisdom eminent,
By patience, temperance."
JOHN MILTON: Paradise Regained, III, ll. 89-94

"But why should man seek glory? Who of his own
Hath nothing, and to whom nothing belongs
But condemnation, ignominy, and shame?
Who for so many benefits receiv'd
Turn'd recreant to God, ingrate and false,
And so of all true good himself despoil'd,
Yet, sacrilegious, to himself would take
That which to God alone of right belongs;
Yet so much bounty is in God, such grace,
That who advance his glory, not their own,
Them he himself to glory will advance."
JOHN MILTON: Paradise Regained, III, ll. 134-144

". . . But patience, to prevent
That murmur, soon replies, God doth not need
Either man's work or his own gifts, who best
Bear his milde yoak, they serve him best, his State
Is Kingly. Thousands at his bidding speed
And post o're Land and Ocean without rest:
They also serve who only stand and waite."

JOHN MILTON: *On His Blindness*

The concept of glory has of late years been seen by Renaissance scholars to be more and more central to the proper understanding and interpretation of much Renaissance literature. Recently Professor Merritt Hughes, in an article entitled "Milton and the Sense of Glory,"[1] explored the concept of glory as it operates in the thought and poetry of Milton, particularly in his *Paradise Regained*. Professor Hughes calls attention, at the beginning of his article, to the strange omission of Milton from Herbert Read's *The Sense of Glory:*

> Exclusion from even the most eclectic survey of the experience of glory in literature from medieval to modern times is strange treatment for Milton, whose theme in every major poem may be regarded on one of its facets as glory.[2]

Although this article has done much to call attention to the importance of this notion in Milton's thought, there is at least one statement in it that suggests some lack of precision on Professor Hughes' part in dealing with Milton's concept of glory and the virtue of magnanimity which is concerned with glory. In one place in the article, he says:

> In actual fact, the Christ of *Paradise Regained* is no more a piece of self-portrayal than is the Christ of *The Christian Doctrine*, II, ix, where he stands as he does in the poem with Job as an example of the Aristotelian virtue of magnanimity,

[161]

or the "acceptance or refusal of riches, advantages, or honors" in accordance with the individual's "own dignity, rightly understood." [3]

Now if there is one thing that is evident from a study of Milton's treatment of glory in *Paradise Lost*, *The Christian Doctrine*, and *Paradise Regained*, it is that it differs fundamentally from that of Aristotle. It is the purpose of this chapter to show that Milton's concept of honor and glory is in many ways a conscious abrogation of the notion as it was described by Aristotle in his discussion of magnanimity. [4]

As I have pointed out in Chapter One, for Aristotle the magnanimous man was a man who excelled in all virtue and who insisted on the honor proportionate to his virtue. Honor was his supreme good. It was what he lived for; everything was subordinate to it. And unlike all other Aristotelian virtues, which consisted of a mean between the opposites of excess and defect, in the case of magnanimity, which was concerned with the rational attitude toward great honors, according to Aristotle, there was no possibility of excess. In practice this meant that there were no limits to the honor and recognition that the truly pre-eminent man could demand. Since by definition he was supposed to be supreme in all virtues—physical, intellectual, and moral—any honor that he claimed was owing to him. He could not be excessive in his claims; and he was willing to sacrifice everything, even life itself, in procuring the honor that he considered his due. This resulted in a self-centeredness, an exaggerated individualism, and a hauteur in the great-souled man as Aristotle describes him that comes close to what a Christian ethics would call pride. My point here is that the very thing that we in a Christian economy would think of as a basis for dishonor is the central motivation of the honor paid the Aristotelian hero.

I have discussed, in greater detail, Aristotle's magnanimous man in Chapter One; I only refer to it here again in order to suggest the caution one must practice in making generalizations about the Aristotelianism of Milton's or almost any other Renaissance writer's concept of glory. It is my contention that what Milton went out of his way to make clear is that his concept of glory represents the specific limitations that Christianity put on the whole subject of the pursuit of glory. As Miss Hulbert[5] and Professor Maloney[6] have shown in the case of Spenser, far better guides than Aristotle in this area are the writings of Saint Thomas Aquinas and other medieval and Renaissance commentators on the ethics of Aristotle.

In the case of Saint Thomas, one has to read carefully to notice the difference between his discussion of magnanimity and that of Aristotle.[7] He retains so much of the verbal elaboration of the *Nicomachean Ethics* that one can miss the fact that by a distinction here and a qualification there, or by an elaborate discussion tucked away in an answer to an objection, he completely changes the whole notion of the virtue. Far from admitting that there is no possibility of excess in the claims for honor on the part of the magnanimous man, Saint Thomas insists that even he can be excessive by either presumption or ambition. He can be presumptuous by attempting something beyond his ability; or he can be excessive in his demands for honor, and that in three ways: (1) by demanding more honor than his virtues actually warrant, thus failing in truthfulness; (2) by claiming it in such a way as to deny his dependence upon God for what he is and does—thus failing in humility; or (3) by claiming it in such a way as to be injurious to his neighbor—thus failing in charity.[8] The Christian, then, can be excessive in his claims for honor, by a fundamental untruthfullness about himself, or by a lack of humility or charity. According to St. Thomas, for the Christian, there *are* things that put a check on even the magnanimous man's pursuit of his own glory—a recognition of his dependence upon God for all that he is and does, and a recognition that he has a duty in charity to use what he has for the benefit of his neighbor as well as for his own self-aggrandizement. According to Saint Thomas, for the Christian, glory is not the end of man's life. He dedicates himself to doing the things, to practicing the virtues, which will bring him honor and glory from God and his fellow men, but not because of the honor accruing from them, but rather because he knows they are the will of God. In this he is like God Himself in creation, who did not create for the honor and glory He would receive from His creatures in their recognition of His excellence manifested in creation. This would be inconsistent with the all-sufficiency of an infinitely perfect being. Rather, His sole purpose in creation was the unselfish manifestation and communication of Himself in creation to man.[9] But man in turn, being a conscious and rational creature and seeing God's excellence manifested in creation, would abuse his rationality if he did not recognize and acknowledge it, if he did not honor and glorify God manifested in His creatures. That is what honor means, after all: the recognition of excellence wherever we find it. In like manner, the Christian, when he is most Christian, does not live virtuously and do great deeds for the honor accruing to this way of acting; on the contrary, he lives virtuously and does great deeds because he knows that they are the will of God and contribute to the welfare of his neighbor and the glory of God. But man, seeing these good deeds, does recognize them, and does honor and glorify the man who does them, but even more the God Who made them possible. This is admittedly a high ideal, and perhaps one not often realized in practice; but my point here is that it is an ideal about as completely different as possible from the Greek ideal formulated by Aristotle in his definition of magnanimity. And it is my further contention that it is this ideal, no matter how or where he came by it, rather than that of Aristotle, that is the background for the central core of Milton's whole concept of the heroic and of his sense of glory in all his prose and poetic works.

When he had finally determined on the Scriptural story of the Fall of Man as the subject matter for his epic, Milton realized that this very subject matter demanded an entirely new formulation of the heroic. If Adam and Eve, his central characters, were to elicit the admiration and honor that their status as epic heroes demanded, it would have to be on a completely different basis from the honor paid to the heroes of traditional epics and romances. We recall his formal abrogation of the traditional concepts of the heroic in the opening lines of Book IX, just before he recounts the tragic disobedience of man:

> That brought into this World a world of woe,
> Sinne and her shadow Death, and Miserie
> Deaths Harbinger.
> —*P.L.*, IX, ll. 11-13.[10]

That, in all conscience, would seem to be an unlikely role in which to cast a hero, and an action least apt to elicit the honor and glory owing an epic hero. Milton himself admits that it is a "sad Task" but goes on immediately to insist that nevertheless it is an argument

> Not less but more Heroic than the wrauth
> Of stern *Achilles* on his Foe pursu'd
> Thrice Fugitive about *Troy* Wall; or rage
> Of *Turnus* for *Lavinia* disespous'd,
> Or *Neptune's* ire or *Juno's* that so long
> Perplex'd the *Greek* and *Cytherea's* Son.
> —*P.L.*, IX, ll. 14-19.

It is worth noting that what Milton is abrogating specifically here as a basis for the heroic or the honorable or admirable is precisely the kind of self-centered pursuit of one's own glory that is exemplified in both Achilles and Turnus. On the other hand, he avoids anything like a criticism of Odysseus and Aeneas, casting them in something like passive roles as victims to the self-centered ire of Neptune and Juno. As a matter of fact, by this very device, Milton is more than suggesting that in the characters of Odysseus and Aeneas we have a vague prototype of the new human ideal "not less but more Heroic than the wrauth of stern *Achilles* . . . or rage of *Turnus* for *Lavinia* disespous'd." It takes Milton the action of the whole twelve books of *Paradise Lost* to reveal to his main characters, Adam and Eve, and through them to us this new ideal, not less but more heroic, actually is. He finally formulates it for us in the last episode of the poem. In Book IX, Eve has listened to the false promises of Satan that she would be like God and perhaps superior to Adam if she ate of the forbidden tree, and Adam has harkened to her and

> . . . scrupl'd not to eat
> Against his better knowledge, not deceiv'd,
> But fondly overcome with Female charm.
> —*P.L.*, IX, ll. 997-999.

Moved by their false ambition to be like gods, Adam and Eve share the forbidden fruit

> . . . and fancie that they feel
> Divinitie within them breeding wings
> Wherewith to scorn the Earth.
> —*P.L.*, IX, ll. 1009-1011.

But they are mistaken; it is only the new movement of concupiscence stirring in their veins that they feel, the first humiliating result of their sin. The sad consequences of their disobedience immediately begin to dawn on Adam:

> O Eve, [he says] in evil hour thou didst give eare
> To that false Worm, of whomsoever taught
> To counterfet Mans voice, true in our Fall,
> False in our promis'd Rising; since our Eyes
> Op'nd we find indeed, and find we know
> Both Good and Evil, Good lost, and Evil got,
> Bad Fruit of Knowledge, if this be to know,
> Which leaves us naked thus, of Honour void,
> Of Innocence, of Faith, of Puritie.
> —*P.L.*, IX, ll. 1067-1075.

[166]

This is only the beginning of a whole procession of mutual
recriminations, that themselves are a manifestation of the chaos
which has been let loose in the universe and in their souls by
their disobedience to the commandment of God, recriminations
that end in despair and Eve's suggestion of suicide. And these
are the people that Milton must remake into Christian heroes.
"Sad task" indeed! It takes all of Books X, XI, and XII, and
an intervention of the Archangel Michael to do it; but by the
end of Book XII the job is done. Humbled by his own fall,
Adam at last sees where his true greatness lies—not in rebellion
against the will of God after the false pattern of Satan, but
by a patient acceptance of the sad consequences of his own
sin, and a hopeful facing of the future, confident in the promise
of a redeemer to come. All of this he expresses in his final reply
to Michael at the end of Book XII:

> Greatly instructed I shall hence depart,
> Greatly in peace of thought, and have my fill
> Of knowledge, what this vessel can containe;
> Beyond which was my folly to aspire.
> Henceforth I learne, that to obey is best,
> And love with feare the onely God, to walk
> As in his presence, ever to observe
> His providence, and on him sole depend,
> Merciful over all his works, with good
> Still overcoming evil, and by small
> Accomplishing great things, by things deem'd weak
> Subverting worldly strong, and worldly wise
> By simply meek; that suffering for Truths sake
> Is fortitude to highest victorie
> And to the faithful Death the Gate of Life;
> Taught this by his example whom I now
> Acknowledge my Redeemer ever blest.
> —*P.L.*, XII, ll. 557-573.

This difficult ideal of obedience, humility, patience, temperance, and love, which Adam and Eve came to recognize at
long last and after much disillusionment, is made even more

emphatic by being contrasted throughout *Paradise Lost* with the disobedience, rebellious pride, and intemperate hatred and jealously of Satan. And, as both C. M. Bowra[11] and C. S. Lewis[12] have pointed out, Milton underlines the contrast by consciously using the old pagan Aristotelian and Achillean concept of heroism raised to archangelic and cosmic proportions as the framework for building up the character of Satan. But there is a sublime irony in all the proud, vaunting, defiant speeches of Satan that cover up a spirit that is "inward wracked with pain," and an even greater irony in Satan's success against mankind, which all culminates in his own complete humiliation and confusion as he returns to Hell to savor this triumph, only to hear himself hissed by the host of fallen angels turned to hideous serpents, all groveling before him as he himself falls

> A monstrous Serpent on his Belly prone,
> Reluctant, but in vaine, a greater power
> Now rul'd him, punisht in the shape he sinn'd.
>   —*P.L.*, X, ll. 514-516.

This is Satan's exit from the poem. This is the reward of his obdurate pride and steadfast hate. The poet could hardly have written the lesson larger.

But it is not only in *Paradise Lost* that Milton touches on the check that patience and humility put upon the pursuit of honor and glory. Like so many other Renaissance writers, he returns to the idea repeatedly. We find him, for instance, discussing the whole idea of magnanimity in Chapter IX of Book II of his *Christian Doctrine*.

> The virtues more peculiarly appropriate to a high station are lowliness of mind and magnanimity. Lowliness of mind consists in thinking humbly of ourselves, and in abstaining from self-commendation, except where occasion requires it. . . . Magnanimity is shown, when in seeking or avoiding, the acceptance or refusal of riches, advantages, or honors, we are actuated by a regard to our own dignity rightly understood.[13]

It is interesting to observe that the very definition of magnanimity itself is here paired with that of humility or lowliness of mind—one of the Christian checks on an exaggerated esteem of one's own honor and reputation. For Milton here magnanimity is as much a norm for rejecting riches, advantages, and honors as for seeking and accepting them. Among a list of Scriptural examples of the acceptance or rejection of riches, power, or honors based on one's own dignity, properly understood, is Christ's rejection of the empires of the world proffered him by Satan. As Professor Hughes has pointed out in the article already cited, this passage in the *Christian Doctrine* is a key to Milton's intentions in *Paradise Regained*, but it should also be a cue to the fact that in *Paradise Regained*, even more clearly than in *Paradise Lost*, a concept of magnanimity totally different from that of Aristotle is guiding the poet.

In *Paradise Regained* we have the pride and deceitfulness of Satan pitted against the New Adam as they were pitted against the Old Adam in *Paradise Lost*. But there the likeness ends. Only at the end of *Paradise Lost*, after the bitter disillusionment from the results of their listening to the false blandishments of Satan, do Adam and Eve learn that their true greatness lies in their humble obedience to the will of God. In *Paradise Regained*, in the person of Christ tempted by Satan, Milton attempts to give a clear picture of unimpeachable Christian magnanimity unshaken by the temptations of Satan. In God the Father's conversation with Gabriel in Book I, Milton's whole purpose in confining himself to the temptations of Christ in *Paradise Regained* is revealed. God the Father refers to Christ's "winning by Conquest what the first man lost/by fallacy surpriz'd" (I, ll. 154-155):

> . . . But first I mean
> To exercise him in the Wilderness,
> There he shall first lay down the rudiments
> Of his great warfare, e're I send him forth

To conquer Sin and Death the two grand foes,
By Humiliation and strong Sufferance.
—*P.R.*, I. ll. 155-160.

In other words, Milton is exploring, in the temptations in *Paradise Regained*, only the rudiments or the fundamental strategy of the pitched battle between Satan and Christ. Milton must have been familiar with the traditional treatment of this battle, which culminated in the rather classic formulation of Saint Ignatius' meditation on the Two Standards in *The Spiritual Exercises*, where the strategies of Satan and Christ in the battle for souls are contrasted. The strategy of Satan, according to Saint Ignatius, is as follows: "The first step shall be that of riches; the second, that of honor; the third, that of pride; and from these three steps he [Satan] draws [men] on to all other vices." [14] This in general is the strategy that Satan follows in the temptations of Christ in *Paradise Regained*. Note, for example, the sequence in the wording of the following ratiocination of Satan:

> Great acts require great means of enterprise,
> Thou art unknown, unfriended, low of birth,
> A Carpenter thy Father known, thy self
> Bred up in poverty and straights at home;
> Lost in a Desert here and hunger-bit:
> Which way or from what hope dost thou aspire
> To greatness? whence Authority deriv'st,
> What Followers, what Retinue canst thou gain,
> Or at thy heels the dizzy Multitude,
> Longer then thou canst feed them on thy cost?
> Money brings Honour, Friends, Conquest, and Realms;
>
> . . . .
>
> Get Riches first, get Wealth, and Treasure heap,
> Not difficult, if thou hearken to me,
> Riches are mine, Fortune is in my hand;
> They whom I favour thrive in wealth amain,
> While Virtue, Valour, Wisdom, sit in want.
> —*P.R.*, II, ll. 411-431.

At another point in the temptations Satan tells Christ that He has perfect goodness, wisdom, and justice, but that He has them to no avail since He refuses to enjoy the fame and glory that they merit for Him. "Glory," says Satan, "is the real motive of high-minded spirits. And you are ripe for the glory of leadership and conquest":

> These God-like Virtues wherefore doest thou hide?
> Affecting private life, or more obscure
> In savage Wilderness, wherefore deprive
> All Earth her wonder at thy acts, Thyself
> The fame and glory, glory the reward
> That sole excites to high attempts the flame
> Of most erected Spirits, most temper'd pure
> Aetherial, who all pleasures else despise,
> All treasures and all gain esteem as dross,
> And dignities and powers all but the highest?
> . . . .
> Quench not the thirst of glory, but augment.
> —*P.R.*, III, ll. 21-38.

This is a voice much like that of Aristotle in the *Nicomachean Ethics*. And Satan cites the example of a host of Achillean heroes from history to bolster his argument—Macedonian Philip, Pompey, Julius Caesar. But Milton has Christ see through the strategy of Satan and confuse him with the reply:

> Thou neither doest persuade me to seek wealth
> For Empires sake, nor Empire to affect
> For Glories sake.
> —*P.R.*, III, ll. 44-46.

A man has true glory and renown, Christ adds,

> When God
> Looking on the Earth, with approbation marks
> The just man, and divulges him through Heaven

> To all his Angels, who with true applause
> Recount his praise.
> —*P.R.*, III, ll. 60-64.

He rejects the false notion of glory based on conquest and battle, and goes on to describe the true basis of glory that echoes the notion developed throughout *Paradise Lost:*

> But if there be in glory ought of good,
> It may by means far different be attain'd
> Without ambition, war, or violence;
> By deeds of peace, by wisdom eminent,
> By patience, temperance.
> —*P.R.*, III, ll. 88-92.

Satan's rejoinder to this is that Christ's Heavenly Father seeks glory, so why shouldn't He? It is in Christ's reply to Satan here that Milton particularly reveals how much he owes to the Christian commentators on Aristotle for his concept of true glory and how foreign his notion of magnanimity is to that of Aristotle. This is Christ's reply:

> And reason; [that God should expect glory from His
>   creatures] since his word all things produc'd
> Though chiefly not for glory as prime end,
> But to shew forth his goodness, and impart
> His good communicable to every soul
> Freely; of whom what could he less expect
> Than glory and benediction, that is thanks,
> The slightest, easiest, readiest recompense
> From them who could return him nothing else,
> And not returning that would likeliest render
> Contempt instead, dishonour, obloquy?
> —*P.R.*, III, ll. 122-131.

This is practically a paraphrase of Saint Thomas' statement and of many other medieval theologians about the end of creation. Saint Thomas' succinct statement is that God's purpose

[172]

in creation was to communicate and manifest His goodness.[15] It was to communicate and manifest His goodness to men that God created, not to receive anything from them. But His goodness, once communicated, elicits the acknowledgment and thanks of rational creatures who see it. "Of whom what could he less expect than glory and benediction," is Milton's way of putting it.

And Milton has Christ go on in his reply to Satan to press home the point that it is this very unself-centered action of God in creation that ought to be the model for men in their attitude toward glory. Whatever they have, they have from God. "What hast thou, that thou hast not received? And if thou hast received, why dost thou glory as if thou hast not received?" Saint Paul phrases it (I Cor. 4:7). Furthermore, Saint Paul says of himself that, since the only thing he has that is truly his own is his sin, this is another reason why there is nothing of his own that merits praise or glory (II Cor. 12). Milton puts almost the same words on the lips of Christ as part of His response to Satan here:

> But why should man seek glory? who of his own
> Hath nothing, and to whom nothing belongs
> But condemnation, ignominy, and shame?
> Who for so many benefits receiv'd
> Turn'd recreant to God, ingrate and false,
> And so of all true good himself despoil'd,
> Yet, sacrilegious, to himself would take
> That which to God alone of right belongs;
> Yet so much bounty is in God, such grace,
> That who advance his glory, not their own,
> Them he himself to glory will advance.
>   —*P.R.*, III, ll. 134-144.

Milton is expressing through Christ here one of the great antinomies of Christianity that runs through Scripture like a refrain: "Every one that exalteth himself, shall be humbled; and he that humbleth himself shall be exalted" (Luke 14:11). It is a point that strikes home even to Satan, who is the living eternal example of the terrible futility of all the excesses against magnanimity—presumption, ambition, and pride:

> and here again
> Satan had not to answer, but stood struck
> With guilt of his own sin, for he himself
> Insatiable of glory had lost all.
> —*P.R.*, III, ll. 145-148.

It should be evident, I think, even from this brief discussion, how central in the thought of Milton, both in *Paradise Lost* and in *Paradise Regained*, is this concept of glory. But it should be equally clear that Milton's idea of magnanimity—that virtue which concerns itself with the rational attitude towards honor and glory—is worlds removed from the Aristotelian concept. The Aristotelian definition is a better guide for understanding the character of Satan in these two poems.[16] He embodies an attitude toward glory that Milton is explicitly repudiating in both poems.

But there is one other point that must be made about Milton's concept of the heroic. As Frank Kermode has pointed out, it clearly smacks of the ancient Stoic ideal of withdrawal from and rejection of [17] the vain pursuits of the world. In *Paradise Lost*, we recall, Milton does reject in order and by name every one of the heroic ideals of the past. His is not a mere qualification of the Aristotelian ideal with the principles of Christian humility and charity—although, as we have seen, he does include these principles in his ideal—but a substitution of the new ideal of patient suffering for the older ones of more active and external achievement. And in *Paradise Regained* his hero Christ is forthright in his cold rejection of the glory that accrues to riches, power, and intellectual pursuits. So much emphasis is put on this note of rejection and the substitution of the new ideal of patient suffering in Milton's discussions of the heroic that it practically amounts to a reassertion of the

Augustinian ideal. Professor Kermode remarks that "the whole poem [*Paradise Regained*] is concerned to establish the character of Christian heroic virtue as distinct from pagan, and to establish the heavenly nature of the rewards which supersede the earthly recompense of the old heroes." [18] Certainly it is rather God's approval and the approval of the angels in heaven and therefore heavenly glory that Milton is thinking of when he speaks of the glory that is won by the new ideal of patient suffering in Adam and Eve, Job, and Christ Himself, rather than any glory on earth. It is one of the many ironies[19] of Milton's literary career that he who had dedicated his life to achieving heroic stature himself as the great English epic poet should evolve in his epics a concept of the heroic that was nine tenths a rejection of the heroic motif. But, in a way, this is not as ironic as it appears at first glance, because, even in his personal ideal, there was much of this element of patient suffering, as his sonnet on his own blindness testifies. "They also serve who only stand and wait." It is this aspect of the Miltonic heroic ideal, then, that separates him measurelessly from the ideals of Aristotle, and even widely from the more moderate view of Saint Thomas, and relates him much more closely to the ascetic view of Saint Augustine.[20] Unlike Spenser, he does not see the pursuit of earthly glory as a means of meriting heavenly glory, except by its rejection and the substitution for it of the completely new ideal of patient suffering. This Stoic and Augustinian coloring in the Miltonic ideal makes the more tolerant view of Spenser stand out with even greater clarity.

NOTES

[1] Merritt Hughes, "Milton and the Sense of Glory," *Philological Quarterly*, XXVIII (1949), 107-124.

[2] *Ibid.*, p. 107.

[3] *Ibid.*, p. 113.

[4] The terms "honor," "glory," and "magnanimity" will keep recurring in this chapter. It might be well, therefore, to state at the outset the sense in which they are used here. They are very closely

related but are not synonymous: *Honor* is the recognition and acknowledgment of excellence wherever it is found. *Glory* adds to that concept a suggestion of signal honor and something of a demonstrative, external manifestation of that honor on the part of a large number. *Magnanimity* is the virtue which is concerned with the rational attitude that the person honored (one, incidentally, who by his pre-eminent excellence deserves *great* honor) takes toward the honor owing to him. See St. Thomas, *Summa Theologica*, II, II^ae, CIII, ad 3, for a discussion of the relationship between honor and glory.

⁵ Viola Blackburn Hulbert, "Spenser's Twelve Moral Virtues 'According to Aristotle and the Rest.'" Unpublished doctoral dissertation, University of Chicago, 1927.

⁶ Michael F. Maloney, "St. Thomas and Spenser's Virtue of Magnificence," *Journal of English and German Philology*, LII (1953), 58-62.

⁷ *Summa Theologica*, II, II^ae, CXXXI, ad Iam. See Chapter Seven for a fuller discussion of Magnanimity in St. Thomas.

⁸ *Ibid.*, corpus.

⁹ In the *Summa Theologica* (I, XLIV, articulus 4, ad corpus) Saint Thomas has this to say about the end of creation: *Primo agenti, qui est agens tantum, non convenit agere propter acquisitionem alicujus finis; sed intendit solum communicare suam perfectionem quae est ejus bonitas. Et unaquaeque creatura intendit consequi suam perfectionem, quae est similitudo perfectionis et bonitatis divinae.* "It is not proper that the first agent who is pure agent should act for the acquisition of any end; but rather it is His sole purpose to communicate His perfection which is His own goodness. And every creature aims at achieving its own perfection which is a likeness to the divine perfection and goodness."

And in the *Summa Contra Gentiles* (Lib. III, cap. xviii) similarly he says: *Oportet quod eo modo effectus tendat in finem quo agens propter finem agit. Deus autem, qui est primum agens omnium rerum, non sic agit quasi sua actione aliquid acquirat, sed quasi sua actione aliquid largiatur, quia non est in potentia ut aliquid acquirere possit, sed solum in actu perfecto ex quo potest aliquid elargiri. Res igitur non ordinantur in Deum sicut in finem cui aliquid acquiratur, sed ut ab ipso ipsumet suo modo consequantur, quum ipsemet sit finis.* "It is necessary that an effect tends to its end in the same manner as the agent acts for an end. But God, Who is the first agent of all things, does not act as if He received anything from His action, but as giving something by it, because He is not in potency to receive anything, but only in perfect act by reason of which He can give something. Things therefore are not directed to God as to an end which can receive something, but in order that they may obtain from Him according to their capacities God Himself, since He is their end."

[10] The quotations from Milton's *Paradise Lost* and *Paradise Regained* are from *The Student's Milton*, edited by Frank Allen Patterson. Copyright 1930, 1933, by Frank Allen Patterson. Reprinted by permission of Appleton-Century-Crofts, Inc. References in the text are to book and line numbers of this edition.

[11] C. M. Bowra, "Milton and the Destiny of Man," *From Virgil to Milton* (London: Macmillan & Co., Ltd., 1945), pp. 227-231.

[12] C. S. Lewis, "Satan," *A Preface to Paradise Lost* (London: Oxford University Press, 1952), pp. 92-101.

[13] Milton, "Christian Doctrine," in *The Student's Milton*, p. 1064. Milton would certainly have had no precedent for his juxtaposition of humility and magnanimity as marks of the great man in Aristotle's *Ethics*, but rather again in Saint Thomas as the following passage from the *Summa Theologica* II, II[ae], CXXIX, ad 4, will show: "There is in man something great which he possesses through the gift of God; and something defective which accrues to him through the weakness of nature. Accordingly magnanimity makes a man deem himself worthy of great things in consideration of the gifts he holds from God: thus if his soul is endowed with great virtue, magnanimity makes him tend to perfect works of virtue; and the same is to be said of the use of any other good, such as science or external fortune. On the other hand, humility makes a man think little of himself in consideration of his own deficiency, and magnanimity makes him despise others in so far as they fall away from God's gifts: since he does not think so much of others as to do anything wrong for their sake. Yet humility makes us honour others and esteem them better than ourselves, in so far as we see some of God's gifts in them. Hence it is written of the just man (Ps. xiv. 4): *In his sight a vile person is contemned*, which indicates the contempt of magnanimity, *but he honoureth them that fear the Lord*, which points to the reverential bearing of

humility. It is therefore evident that magnanimity and humility are not contrary to one another, although they seem to tend in contrary directions, because they proceed according to different considerations."

[14] Ignatius Loyola, *The Spiritual Exercises*, translated by Father Elder Mullan, S.J. (New York: P. J. Kenedy and Sons, 1914), p. 75. There was, of course, a long tradition for representing the strategy of Satan in these steps—riches, honor, pride—in homiletic and devotional literature. One of the earliest manifestations of it in English literature is in the homily on humility delivered by Hrothgar at the end of the second episode in *Beowulf*.

[15] See note 9.

[16] C. M. Bowra is emphatic about Milton's intention in regard to Satan in relationship to the traditional heroic ideal: "It is clear that Milton quite deliberately fashioned Satan on heroic models, because he rejected the old heroic standards and wished to show that they were wicked. He had his own ideal of heroism, which he displays in other ways, and his Satan prepares us for it by showing that pride, on which the old ideal was based, is not only inadequate but dangerously wrong."—*Op. cit.*, p. 229.

[17] See Frank Kermode, "Milton's Hero," *The Review of English Studies*, new series, IV (1953), 317-330.

[18] *Ibid.*, p. 329.

[19] There are other ironies in Milton's literary career. It has always struck me as ironic that, in *Samson Agonistes*, a play which Milton calls a tragedy after the Greek manner, he invites us not to pity his hero but to admire him for his confusion of his enemies and that, in *Paradise Lost*, which he conceives as his great epic, he moves us in the last scene, to pity rather than admiration for the characters of Adam and Eve, as hand in hand they take their solitary way out of the Garden of Paradise.

[20] Edwin B. Benjamin would seem to agree with this interpretation of Milton's view of glory as is evidenced in the following quotation: "As *Lycidas* would suggest, Milton would never have made earthly fame an ultimate goal in itself, but at the same time there seems to be in his later works a growing rejection of Fame in favor of the absolute values of religion."—*Op. cit.*, p. 83.

Honour is flashed off exploit, so we say;
And those strokes once that gashed flesh or galled
*   shield*
Should tongue that time now, trumpet now that field,
And, on the fighter, forge his glorious day.
On Christ they do and on the martyr may;
But be the war within, the brand we wield
Unseen, the heroic breast not outward-steeled,
Earth hears no hurtle then from fiercest fray.

*   Yet God (that hews mountain and continent,*
Earth, all, out; who, with trickling increment,
Veins violets and tall trees makes more and more)
Could crowd career with conquest while there went
Those years and years by of world without event
That in Majorca Alfonso watched the door.

GERARD MANLEY HOPKINS:
In Honour of St. Alphonsus Rodriguez,
Laybrother of the Society of Jesus[1]

[1] From *Poems of Gerard Manley Hopkins,* third edition, edited by W. H. Gardner. Copyright 1948 by Oxford University Press, Inc. Reprinted by permission.

This study began, I must confess, in an effort to pinpoint the generalizations that have sometimes been made about the Christian spirit of *Beowulf*. It very soon became evident, as the study progressed, that a very helpful way of making the Christian character of Beowulf more apparent would be to compare him with the characters of the great pagan epics that preceded him. Most previous studies that have compared *Beowulf* with

The Aeneid have concerned themselves primarily with the possible influence of the classical epic form on the Anglo-Saxon poem; very little attention has been given to the ways in which the character of Beowulf himself differs from that of almost any of the great classical epic heroes. There is admittedly a great deal of the traditionally heroic, especially of the Nordic heroic, that still clings to the slayer of Grendel and the dragon; but there is also a great deal both in his fundamental character and actions and in those of Hrothgar that is imbued with the new spirit of Christian humility and charity which makes the differences between *Beowulf* and the classical epics more striking than any resemblances that can be indicated. The comparative study of the three epic characters of Greek, Roman, and Nordic origins and of the philosophical formulations of the heroic ideals which they embody makes the specifically Christian qualities of Beowulf much more apparent.

Within the Christian tradition itself, there developed divergent attitudes toward the whole subject of the pursuit of earthly glory which have perhaps been best formulated by Saint Augustine and Thomas Aquinas. In the Augustinian view, any concern for earthly glory was looked upon with suspicion; while, in the more balanced view of Aquinas, earthly glory could be the concern of even a Christian as long as he pursued it with due humility and charity. In the area of the English epic, we have seen that Spenser's view of earthly glory inclines to the more moderate view of Aquinas, whereas Milton's ultimately shows greater affinities to that of Augustine.

But this study has a significance far beyond the light it throws on the Christian aspects of *Beowulf* and the other English epics. It brings into focus three concepts of human greatness that have always contended and continue to contend with one another for ascendancy in the history of the West—what might be called the Greek, the Roman, and the Christian ideals. The Greek ideal tends to be exaggeratedly individualistic and self-centered; the Roman ideal, on the contrary, is exaggeratedly social, tending to subordinate the individual to society or

[180]

the State; while the Christian ideal attempts to preserve the best elements of both the Greek and Roman ideals, but gives new dignity to the individual as a child of God and puts a check on his unlimited self-aggrandizement by clarifying his dependence upon God and his duty to his fellow men and by orienting his whole life to a clearly conceived destiny beyond time. It expands the Roman notion of social duty into the new concept of Christian charity. Achilles, Aeneas, Beowulf, the Redcrosse Knight, Adam, and the Christ of *Paradise Regained*, this study has shown, are fair approximations of the idea of the great man as certain moments of the Greek, Roman, and Christian societies in turn have conceived him.

It would be very rewarding to pursue further than this study has done the vicissitudes of the magnanimous man, to trace, in other words, what society, under ever-changing political, social, economic, and religious circumstances, has considered an honorable or admirable man to be. Different as the medieval knight, the Renaissance courtier, and the gentleman of later centuries were, they were the men that their respective societies looked up to as their heroes.

Interestingly enough, a broad view of the history of Western civilization shows that, in this ever-shifting concept of the honorable man, there has been a constant recurrence of the emphases we have observed here in the Greek, Roman, and early Christian Eras. Exaggerated individualism, on the one hand, and exaggerated statism on the other, with an attempt on the part of Christianity to check, elevate, and transform both exaggerations with the new virtues of humility and charity, do in a very broad way spell out certain cycles of the history of the West. Where Christianity has failed in its moderating task, as it has intermittently, the failure is partly owing to the fact that it has in some of its members allowed itself to be for a time a carrier of the very values it has a commission to transform. This is, in part, the story of the late Middle Ages and the Renaissance and of nineteenth-century liberalism. It would be interesting to trace in detail, both in theoretic statement and in literary image, the cyclic return of the sequence of values we have traced here in the epics. Such a study would end in a contrast between the current counterpulls between the very assertive individualism of contemporary existentialist philosophy and literature and the equally compelling tendency to conformism which figures so broadly in the life and literature of the modern era. It is still the task of Christianity today to accept what is best in these current forms of individualism and other-mindedness, and transform them into an image of human greatness that preserves the integrity and perfection of the individual but an integrity and perfection partly realized by an other-minded service of one's neighbor. Such a study deserves doing, but it would demand another book, and one more extensive than the present volume, to achieve it. Such a book would give additional evidence that honor in every age is far more than Falstaff's "mere scutcheon."

INDEX

Abbot Melitus, 81

Achilles, xiii, 52, 54, 55, 56, 57, 60, 61, 63, 64, 65, 66, 68, 72, 73, 74, 86, 91, 92, 93, 106, 107, 165, 166, 168, 181; Greek magnanimous man, 8-32; not tragic 8, 10, 30, 31, 32, 33; heroic stature, 11; contrasted with Ajax, Odysseus, Menelaus, Hector, 10-13; conscious of his own superiority, 13; attitude toward fellow Achaeans, 13-14; personal honor, persistent motive, 14-22; honor based on prowess in battle, 23-24, 71; not criticized for demands for honor, 24-30; pathetic, 30-31

Acrasia, 158

Adam, new heroic ideal of patience, 166, 167, 169, 181

Aeneas, 109, 154, 165, 181; *in Iliad*, 12; Roman magnanimous man, 51-69, exemplifies Roman hierarchy of virtues, 51, 55, 61; high sense of duty, 51-61; *paterfamilias*, 61; peace rather than war, 61-64, 71; hatred of deceit, 64; hatred of cruelty, 65; subordination of individual to state, 67; sacrifice of Dido and Turnus, 67

Aeneid, 51-69, 180; central theme —sense of duty, 51-61; peace rather than war glorified, 61-64, 71

Agamemnon, 9, 10, 12, 13, 14, 15, 17, 18, 19, 21, 24, 25, 26, 27, 28, 29, 30, 32, 33, 35, 36, 38, 39

Ajax, 11, 13, 29, 35, 38

Alecto, 62, 71, 72

Amata, 62, 71

ambition, *in Aristotle:* not excess against magnanimity, 4; Menelaus, example of, 12; *in Thomas Aquinas:* excess against magnanimity, 126, 128, 133; *in More's Utopia:* 132; Wolsey example of, 132; *in Spenser's Mother Hubberds Tale:* 138-142; Ape and Foxe as examples of, 140-141; *in Philotime of The Faerie Queene:* 142-144, 158; *in Milton's Paradise Lost:* 166

Amphinomus, 37

An Inquisition upon Fame and Honour, 131

Anchises, 55, 57, 58, 59, 60, 61, 154

Andromache, 34, 35

Antilochus, 19

Antinous, 37

Antonius, 150

Ape and Foxe, 148; of *Mother Hubberds Tale*, example of ambition, 138-144

Apollo, 9, 16

Archimago, 147, 148

Aristotle, vii, xi, xii, 123, 126, 128, 138, 142, 145, 156, 157, 161, 162, 163, 164, 168, 169, 171, 172, 174, 175, 177; discussion of magnanimous man, 1-4; concept of virtue, 53

Arthur, 151, 157; example of magnanimity or true pursuit of

glory, 144; relationship to magnificence, 145; as sanctifying grace, 148
Ascanius, 55, 57, 60
Astyanax, 34
Ate, 30
Athene, 16, 37, 38
Augustus, 70

Benjamin, Edwin B., 135, 158, 178
Beowulf, xiii, 107-108, 179, 180, 181; Christian hero, 87-109; example of Christian magnanimous man, 89, 90, 109; pre-eminent in all virtues, 90-91; humility, 93-100; charity, 100-103; prowess in battle, 108-109
Beowulf, 84, 119, 178, 179, 180; an allegory of salvation, 85; substantially Christian, 87-89; multiple authorship, 86, 110
"*Beowulf*, An Allegory of Salvation?" 85
Beowulf: An Introduction to the Study of the Poem with a Discussion of Offa and Finn, 110
Beowulf and the Fight at Finnsburg, 110
Beowulf and the Finnesburg Fragment, a Translation into Modern English Prose, 110
"*Beowulf* and the 'Heroic Age' in England," 110
"*Beowulf*: The Monsters and the Critics," 112, 117
Beowulf, The Oldest English Epic, 110
Boccaccio, 129
Bowra, C. M., 32, 53, 63, 69, 71, 72, 168, 177, 178
"brave Courtier," example of Spenser's magnanimous man, 139-140

Briseis, 9, 18, 27, 35
On Britain and Germany, 85
Butcher, Samuel Henry, 30

Caelia, 152, 153
Caesar, 61, 70
casus virorum illustrium, 150
Cave of Error, 147
Chadwick, Hector Monroe, 88
Chambers, R. W., 87, 88, 110
Charissa, 152, 156
charity, *in Cicero:* 42-46; *in Saint Paul:* 77-78; *in Saint Gregory the Great:* 82-83; *in Saint Augustine:* 119-123; *in Saint Thomas Aquinas:* 127-128, 147; *in Spenser:* 151-153; *in Milton:* 168-169
Chaucer, attitude toward honor and earthly fame, 128-129
Christ, 76, 181; new ideal—humility and charity, 76-77; *in Paradise Regained:* new heroic ideal, in Christ tempted, 169-174
The Christian Doctrine, 161, 162, 168, 177
Christian magnanimous man, 75-83; pursuit of honor limited by humility and charity, 76-77; new emphasis on dignity of individual, 78; Roman antecedents, 80; Nordic antecedents, 80; *in Saint Paul's Epistles*, 75-79; *in Saint Thomas Aquinas*, 123-128; *in Spenser*, 145; *in Milton's Paradise Lost*, 161-168; *in Paradise Regained*, 169-173
Christian Mysticism in the Elizabethan Age with Its Background in Mystical Methodology, 158
Chryseis, 9
Cicero, 64, 77; discussion of magnanimous man, 40-50

Circe, 109
The City of God, 132, 133
City of God, 120, 122, 123, 135
City of Man, 120, 122, 123, 135
Cleopatra, 150
Cleopolis, 153, 154
Clytemnestra, 21
Colet, John, 132
Collins, Joseph B., 158
comedy, vii
congruity, in the epic, x
Cooper, Lane, 30
Cornford, Francis M., 50, 133
Creusa, 54, 73

death, Greek attitude toward, 7
De Casibus Virorum Illustrium, 129
De Oficiis, 41, 64
De Selincourt, E., 157
"The Degradation of the Red Cross Knight," 158
Deucalion, 23
Dido, 52, 53, 55, 57, 59, 60, 67, 70, 72, 73
Diomedes, 29, 38
Dioscuri, example of Stoic Virtue, 69
Drayton, Michael, 158
Duessa, 148, 151
duty, *in Cicero*: 42-46, 49; *in Virgil's Aeneid*: 51-61
Dwarfe, natural temperance, 147, 150

The Ecclesiastical History of Britain, 81-83, 85
Echeclus, 23
English Literary History, 157, 158
epic, x
Epistle to Corinthians I and II, 77-79, 119
Epistle to the Ephesians, 70

Ethica Nicomachea, 5, 6
Eumaeus, 37
Eve, 166, 167, 169
Exegi monumentum aere perennius, 130

The Faerie Queene, 157; magnanimity in, 140-156; in Arthur, 144-145
Falstaff, 182
fame, *in Chaucer*: 128, 135; *in Italian Renaissance figures*: 130; *in Petrarch*: 130; *in Feltham*: 131; *in Fulke Greville*: 131; *in Middle Ages and Renaissance generally*: 135; *in Spenser*: 138, 156, 157, 158-159
"Fame, Poetry, and the Order of History in the Renaissance," 135, 158
fear of death, 7
Feltham, Owen, 131, 135
Fidelia, 152
Fortune, 128, 135
From Virgil to Milton, 69, 177

Gardner, W. H., 179
Germania, 80
Gloriana, 144, 145, 146, 154, 156, 157, 158
glory, *in The Iliad*: 8, 29; *in Saint Paul*: 76-79; earthly and heavenly *in Saint Augustine*: 120-123; earthly glory amongst pagans according to Augustine, 120; best to suppress desire of, 122; *in the Middle Ages in general*: 128-129, 135; *in the Italian Renaissance*: 129-130, 135; *in the North*: 130-133, 135; *in Feltham*: 131; *in Fulke Greville*: 131; *in Thomas More*: 132; *in Spenser's*

Faerie Queene: earthly glory, 138, 144-156; Gloriana, example of true, 144; Arthur, example of true, 145-146; Redcrosse Knight, motivated by, 146; true relationship between earthly and heavenly, 146-156, 153-154; earthly glory not identified with pride in Spenser, 148; glory of Heavenly Jerusalem, 153; heavenly glory merited by pursuit of glory in active life, 155; pursuit limited by humility and charity, 156; *in Milton:* totally different from Aristotle's notion, 163; based on Thomas Aquinas, 163-164; new concept, 165-168; in the temptations of Christ, 170-174; relation of earthly to heavenly glory, 175, 178; general definition, 176

Greenlaw, Edwin A., 157

Grendel, 87, 92, 93, 95, 96, 101, 103, 105, 109, 180

Greville, Fulke, 131, 136

Haecker, Theodor, 70

Hall, Clark, 88, 110, 112

Healy, John, 133

Hebrew people, 76

Hector, 12, 13, 14, 15, 17, 18, 22, 25, 30, 33, 35, 36, 52, 56, 65, 108; also Aristotle's magnanimous man, 34

Helen, 57

Helenus, 59

Heorot, 94, 105, 116

Hephaestus, 11, 16

hereafter, Greek attitude toward, 3, 7

Hercules, example of Stoic virtue, 69

Heremod, 99, 115

Heroic Age, 88

Homer, concept of magnanimous man, 8-32, 63, 66, 74

honor, vi; *in Saint Paul:* 76-79; twofold attitude toward in Christian tradition, 119; *in Saint Augustine:* 119-123; *in Saint Thomas Aquinas:* 123-128, 133, 163-164; *in Plato:* 119-120; severer view of Augustine prevailed in Middle Ages, 128; *in Feltham:* 131; *in Fulke Greville:* 131; *in Spenser's Mother Hubberds Tale:* 138-142; *in The Faerie Queene:* 144-156; Gloriana, true honor, 144; general definition, 176

Hopkins, Gerard Manley, 179

Horace, 130

Hospital of Mercie, 152

Hotspur, vi

The House of Fame, 128, 135

House of Holiness, 151, 156, 158; school of humility and charity, 152-153

House of Pride, 148-151, 152

Hrothgar, 87, 88, 91, 92, 93; humility and dependence on God, 96-97; exhorts Beowulf to humility, 98-99, 100, 102, 103; wisdom of age, 104; excels in humility and charity, 105; gentleness, 106; prowess in battle, 108, 115, 116, 178, 180

Hughes, Merritt, 161, 169

Hulbert, Viola, 157, 163

humility, *in Saint Paul:* 77-78; *in Saint Gregory the Great:* 82-83; *in Saint Augustine:* 119-123; *in Saint Thomas Aquinas:* 124, 127-128, 147; *in Spenser:* 151-153, 156; *in Milton:* 166-174

Humiltá, 152, 156

Hygd, 88

Hygelac, 100, 102

Iliad, 8-32, 67, 69, 74, 86; not tragic, 8, 10, 31, 33; central theme, 9-11; more primitive ideal than that in Aristotle, 23; pathetic, 31; tragic, 32-33, 54
Il Principe, 130
incongruity, in comedy, viii; in tragedy, ix
In Honour of St. Alphonsus Rodriguez, 179
An Inquisition upon Fame and Honour, 131

Journal of English and Germanic Philology, 85, 157, 176
Julius Caesar, 171
Juno, 51, 72, 165
Jupiter, 56, 57, 59, 61

Kennedy, Charles W., 87, 89, 110
Kermode, Frank, 174, 175, 178
Klaeber, Frederic, 87, 109, 110, 115, 116

Laertes, 37
Latinus, 62, 63, 66
Lavinia, 62, 66, 165
Lavinium, 51, 56, 59, 62
Leonardo da Vinci, 130
"The Letter to Sir Walter Raleigh," 157
Lewis, C. S., 68, 73, 168, 177
literary genres, vii
love, motive in *The Faerie Queene*, 146, 157
Lucifera, 149-150, 151, 152, 153, 158
l'uomo universale, 130
Lycidas, 178
Lydgate, John, 129

Machiavelli, 130

Mackail, J. W., 68
magnanimity, *in Aristotle:* xii, 1-4; *in Cicero:* 40-49; *in Saint Thomas Aquinas:* 123-128; *in Spenser:* theme of *The Faerie Queene*, 144; relationship to magnificence in Thomas Aquinas and Spenser, 145; *in Milton:* in *Paradise Lost*, 161-168; in *Christian Doctrine*, 168-169; in *Paradise Regained*, 169-173, 174; general definition, 176
magnanimous man, xii; *in Aristotle:* 1-4; definition, 1, 6; relationship to fellow men, 2, 6; attitude toward wealth and power, 3, 6; attitude toward physical prowess and courage, voice, speech, gait, 4; attitude toward death, 7; Achilles model of, 9; attitude toward friends, 2, 13, 123; *in Cicero:* 40-50; definition, 41-45; relationship to fellow men—duty and justice, 42-46; duty to commonweal, 44; hierarchy of duties, 46, 49; attitude toward war, 47-48, 50; attitude toward truth of spoken word, 48; attitude toward friendship, 46, 49, 50; *in Saint Paul:* 75-79; emphasis on humility and charity, 77-78; *in Saint Gregory the Great:* 80-84; respect for native traditions, 81; emphasis on humility and charity, 82-83; *in Saint Augustine:* 119-123; *in Saint Thomas Aquinas:* 123-128; emphasis on humility, 124; attitude toward fellow men, 125-126; humility and charity, limitations on pursuit of honor, 127-128, 147; definition of, 133; *in Spenser:* 138-156; "brave Courtier," first draft

of, 139-140; *in Faerie Queene:* 144-156; Arthur, example of, 144-145; Redcrosse Knight, example of, 147, 154-156; *in Milton:* in *Paradise Lost,* abrogation of old ideal, 165; new ideal in Adam, 166-167; contrasted with old ideal in Satan, 167-168; *in Christian Doctrine:* humility and charity limitations on pursuit of honor, 168, 169; *in Paradise Regained:* Christ in temptations, example of new ideal, 169-174; *in modern scene:* 181-182

magnificence, 144; Arthur, example of, 145

Maloney, Michael, 145, 157, 163

Malvenu, 152

Mammon, 142, 143, 144

Man's Unconquerable Mind, 110

The Meaning of Spenser's Fairyland, 135, 157

mediocre man, *in Aristotle:* 4, 7; *in Thomas Aquinas,* 126; *in Spenser's Mother Hubberds Tale,* 138

Menelaus, 12, 34

Mercury, 59

Meriones, 36

Merlin, 144

Michael the Archangel, 167

Michelangelo, 130

Midsummer Night's Dream, vii

Miller, Walter, 49

Milton, John, 180; on the magnanimous man, 161-175

"Milton and the Destiny of Man," 177

"Milton and the Sense of Glory," 161, 175

"Milton's Hero," 178

Mirror for Magistrates, 129

Monk's Tale, 129

Mother Hubberds Tale, ambition in, 138-144, 148, 150, 157

Mount of Contemplation, 153-154, 156, 158

Mulius, 23

Mullan, S. J., Elder, 178

"Nature and Grace in *The Faerie Queene,*" 157

Nautes, 60

Neill, Kerby, 158

Neoptolemus, 65, 66

Neptune, 165

Nestor, 20, 27, 28, 29

Nicomachean Ethics, 163, 171

O'Connor, Mary Elizabeth, 157

Odysseus, 8, 12, 13, 16, 19, 20, 21, 22, 27, 28, 35, 36, 37, 38, 54, 64, 65, 109, 165

Odyssey, 19, 30, 36, 37, 50, 54, 65, 86

Ogden, H. V. S., 136

Orgoglio, 148; spiritual pride, 151

Panthea, 154

Paradise Lost, xiii, 162; new heroic ideal in, 164-168, 178

Paradise Regained, 161, 162, 181; new heroic ideal in Christ tempted, 169-174

pater familias, 55, 58, 61

patience, new heroic ideal, 167

Patroclus, 10, 13, 14, 15, 16, 18, 19, 31, 33, 34, 39

Patterson, Frank Allen, 177

Pax Romana, 61

Penelope, 37

Petrarch, 130

Philip of Macedonia, 171

Philological Quarterly, 175

Philotime, 148, 158; example of ambition, 142-144

Phoenix, 27, 29, 38
Pius, Aeneas, 51, 69, 70-71
Plato, vii, 5, 41, 50, 119, 133
Pluto, 149
Poems of Gerard Manley Hopkins, 179
Poetics, vii, 9, 30
Polites, 65, 73
Poliziano, 135
Polydamas, 34
Polyphemus, 109
Pompey, 150, 171
Poseidon, 12, 25, 52, 69
Post, L. A., 32
A Preface to Paradise Lost, 73, 177
presumption, 126
Priam, 14, 31, 32, 54, 57, 65, 73
pride, in Saint Augustine: 121-122; in More's Utopia: 132; in Gregory the Great: 134-135; in Spenser's Faerie Queene: 147; masque of, 148; House of Pride, 148; Orgoglio, spiritual pride, 148, 151; in Milton's Paradise Lost: Satan's pride, 169
Proceedings of the British Academy, 112
Proserpina, 149
Puck, viii
pusillanimity, 2, 7, 128
pusillanimous man, 4, 76, 128

Raleigh, Sir Walter, letter to, 144
Rathborne, Isabel E., 134, 148, 157, 158
Read, Herbert, 161
Redcrosse Knight, 142, 181; magnanimity in, 146-156; complete human situation—natural and supernatural, 146; glory his motive, 146; degradation of, 147; unmoved in House of Pride, 149-151; in dungeon of Orgoglio,

157; in the House of Holiness, 151-153; in the Hospital of Mercie, 152; on Mount of Contemplation, 153-154
The Republic, 5, 41, 50, 133
Resolves: Divine, Moral, Political, 135
The Review of English Studies, 178
Rhigmus, 23
Rieu, E. V., 33, 36
Ross, W. B., 4, 5, 6

Saint Alphonsus Rodriguez, 179
Saint Augustine (of England), 80, 81, 82, 84, 93, 154
Saint Augustine (of Hippo), 119-123, 138, 148, 156, 158, 175, 180
Saint George, heavenly glory, 154, 155
Saint Gregory, 80, 81, 82, 83, 84, 93
Saint Ignatius, 170, 178
Saint John, 84
Saint Paul, 70, 76, 83, 90, 93, 109, 119, 173; emphasis on humility and charity, 77-79
Saint Thomas Aquinas, discussion of magnanimity, 123-128, 133, 138, 141, 145, 156, 157, 163, 172, 175, 176-177, 180
"Saint Thomas and Spenser's Virtue of Magnificence," 157
Saint Thomas More, 132, 136
Samson Agonistes, 178
Sansfoy, 158
Satan, xiii, 169; fashioned after old heroic ideal, 167; foil for Adam, 168; temptations of Christ, 170-174, 178
Scamander, 36
Secretum, 130
Semiramnis, 150

The Sense of Glory, 161
Shakespeare, vi
Sigfrit, 87
Sinon, 64
Sir Guyon, 142, 143, 144, 147
Sir Walter Raleigh, letter to, 144
Smith, J. A., 5
Smith, J. C., 157
Spenser, Edmund: on ambition, 138-144; on magnanimity, 145; on the magnanimous man, 133-156; on fame, 138, 156, 157, 158-159; on glory, 138-156, 175, 180; on honor, 144-156
"Spenser's Twelve Moral Virtues 'According to Aristotle and the Rest,'" 157
Speranza, 152
The Spiritual Exercises, 170, 178
Sonnet on His Blindness, 175
Stanford, W. B., 37
Stoicism, 40, 53, 69, 70, 174, 175
Studies in Spenser's Historical Allegory, 157
Studies in the Renaissance, 135
"A Study of the Failure of Spenser's *Mother Hubberds Tale* as a Beast Fable," 157
Summa Contra Gentiles, 176-177
Summa Theologica, 124, 126, 133, 134, 135, 176-177
Sychaeus, 73

Tacitus, 80, 85
Telemachus, 37
teleology in Aristotle, vii

Thersites, 26
Thetis, 10, 11, 13, 22, 25, 31, 36, 39
three ways of spiritual life, 152, 158
Timon, 144
Tolkien, J. R. R., 112, 113, 114, 117
tragedy, ix
trionfi, 130
Trojan horse, 37, 50
Tros, 23
Turnus, 54, 62, 63, 66, 67, 71, 72, 73, 108, 165, 166

The Ulysses Theme, 36
Una, 147, 148, 151, 156
Unferth, 106, 107, 108
Utopia, 132, 136

vanitas vanitatum, 138
Vanity, 126, 128
The Venerable Bede, 81-83, 85, 119
Venus, 52, 56, 61
Virgil, 145; his concept of the magnanimous hero, 51-69; as war poet, 71
Virgil, Father of the West, 71

Wealhtheow, 88, 92, 102
Wiglaf, 96
Wolsey, Cardinal, 132
Woodhouse, A. S. P., 157
Wulfstan, 91

Xanthus, 11

Zeus, 10, 15, 16, 24, 25, 28, 29, 30